SEAFURRERS

The Ships' Cats Who Lapped and Mapped the World

AN INCIDENTAL HISTORY

PHILIPPA SANDALL

Illustrated by Ad Long

THE EXPERIMENT
NEW YORK

SEAFURRERS: *The Ships' Cats Who Lapped and Mapped the World*
Copyright © 2018 by Philippa Sandall
Illustrations copyright © 2018 by Ad Long unless otherwise noted in the Permissions
Acknowledgments starting on page 227, a continuation of this copyright page.

The Experiment, LLC | 220 East 23rd Street, Suite 600 | New York, NY 10010-4658
theexperimentpublishing.com

Many of the designations used by manufacturers and sellers to distinguish their products are
claimed as trademarks. Where those designations appear in this book and The Experiment was
aware of a trademark claim, the designations have been capitalized.

The Experiment's books are available at special discounts when purchased in bulk for premiums
and sales promotions as well as for fund-raising or educational use. For details, contact us at info@
theexperimentpublishing.com.

Library of Congress Cataloging-in-Publication Data

Names: Sandall, Philippa, author.
Title: Seafurrers : the ships' cats who lapped and mapped the world / Philippa
    Sandall and Ad Long.
Description: New York, NY : The Experiment, [2018] | Includes bibliographical
    references.
Identifiers: LCCN 2017047334 (print) | LCCN 2017056969 (ebook) | ISBN
    9781615194384 (ebook) | ISBN 9781615194377 (cloth)
Subjects: LCSH: Cats. | Human-animal relationships. | Seafaring life.
Classification: LCC SF442 (ebook) | LCC SF442 .S26 2018 (print) | DDC
    636.80092/9--dc23
LC record available at https://lccn.loc.gov/2017047334

ISBN 978-1-61519-437-7
Ebook ISBN 978-1-61519-438-4

Text design by Sarah Smith, based on designs by Clare Forte and Ky Long
Cover design by Sarah Schneider
Front cover illustration by Ad Long; cover photo © Robert Bahou | offset.com
Back cover photo, Sydney, circa 1910, by Samuel Hood/Australian National Maritime Museum

Manufactured in China

First printing April 2018
10 9 8 7 6 5 4 3 2 1

Sailor with pet cats sitting on hatch cover, Sydney, Australia, circa 1910

Contents

Preface

Whine the many extraordinary exploits and achievements of the seafarers who lapped and mapped the world are well documented, those of their indispensable pest controllers, shipmates, and mascots are not, apart from a few celebs you will read about here. These famed felines include the intrepid Trim, who circumnavigated Australia with Matthew Flinders; the invaluable Mrs. Chippy, who weathered Antarctic blizzards while keeping watch on Ernest Shackleton's *Endurance*; and the redoubtable Simon of the *Amethyst*, who maintained his pest-control duties day in, day out despite being seriously injured in the Yangtze Incident. Hence this incidental seafurring history, a somewhat flotsam-and-jetsam maritime miscellany drawing on letters, diaries, memoirs, newspaper reports, and photographs to shed new light on life on the ocean waves in the days of sail and steam. We felines favor the oral tradition of storytelling, as you may be aware, so to help me pull this together and put it down on the page, I roped in the indispensable services of a scribe (Philippa Sandall) and illustrator (Ad Long). The views and commentary, of course, are all my own and are signposted throughout: "According to Bart."

I am from a seafurring family. My name, Bart, is a nod to our family hero, the courageous Portuguese explorer and navigator Bartolomeu Dias de Novais, who was given instructions "to sail southwards and on to the place where the sun rises and to continue as long as it was possible to do so" in 1487. First to round the Cape of Good Hope was his claim to fame. ("European" and "as far as we know" should probably be added to this.) Dias sailed out of Lisbon, headed down the west coast of Africa, rounded the Cape, and made it into the Indian Ocean—gateway to the Orient and its riches—and then safely back home. Round trip: sixteen months and seventeen days. There were plenty of rough patches, but homeward bound the Cape took the cake. *Cabo das Tormentas* (Cape of Storms) was what he wrote on the charts. Back in Lisbon, armchair traveler King John II claimed naming rights and plumped for *Cabo da Boa Esperança* (Cape of Good Hope), in hot anticipation of pepper profits and the lucrative spice trade with India. But that was not to be, at least not for another decade and another king.

Christopher Columbus stole the limelight in the interim. He headed west for the spices of the East in 1492 and "found" the New World. What that really means is he sailed across the Atlantic, dropped anchor in the Bahamas, staked the Castile Crown's claim, called the fiery chile that the locals ate *pepper*, and to his dying day never admitted he hadn't "found" what he was looking for. As an unknown and unkind critic aptly put it: "When he started out he didn't know where he was going. When he got to the New World he didn't know where he was. And when he got back to Spain he didn't know where he had been."

Vasco da Gama knew exactly where he was going on his passage to India in 1497–98, and Portugal got its sea route to the East Indies and a monopoly on the profitable spice trade for the next hundred years or so, until the determined emergence of Dutch maritime power, seemingly from nowhere, changed the game again.

But not one of them—Dias, Columbus, or da Gama, nor the explorers and traders who followed—could have done it without the onboard protection against pests for their provisions and cargoes that their able-bodied seafurrers tirelessly provided. How do we know ships' cats played such a key role? The Portuguese carved it in stone, as you can see on this sixteenth-century decorative column in the cloisters of the Jerónimos Monastery in Belém, Lisbon.

BART

A watchful seafurrer stretched out on a square knot, carved on a column of the sixteenth-century Jerónimos Monastery in Lisbon. Today, the monastery's west wing houses the Maritime Museum.

A seaman enticing the ship's cat up one of the shrouds of *Pommern*, a four-masted barque and windjammer operating on the grain trade route between Australia and England during the interwar years, and now anchored behind the Åland Maritime Museum as a display

Embarking

🐈 ACCORDING TO BART

To begin at the beginning, I guess I need to explain how our feline forebears stepped out of the wild and became the sea cats who lapped and mapped the world. It all began some twelve thousand years ago, when *Homo sapiens* (whom I'll call *sapiens* from now on to keep it simple) embraced a change that changed everything. They quit their nomadic hunter-gatherer way of life in various parts of the world and, with a natural eye for real estate, picked out prime locations by lakes and rivers with plenty of freshwater to settle down.

In the Fertile Crescent they built houses, planted seeds of local grasses such as barley and wheat, and kept a few animals around. It was a struggle, but they stuck to it, found their green thumbs, and one day discovered they were harvesting bumper crops of beans, peas, lentils, barley, and wheat and storing the surplus in granaries to put food on the table in lean times. *Sapiens* were now farmers.

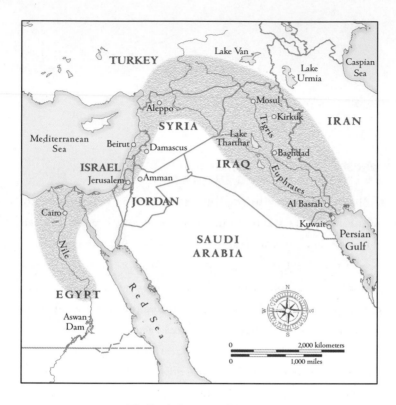

The Fertile Crescent and Nile Valley

Change, *sapiens* found, was constant, as those small settlements grew into villages, towns, cities, empires, and even civilizations, with an ever-increasing number of hungry mouths to feed. Their grain was much more than a vital food source—it was a valuable commodity for barter and trade. *Sapiens* were in business.

But there was a fly in the ointment. *Mus musculus* muscled in for a piece of the action. To a house mouse, the farmers' fields of ripening grain must have looked like an open invitation to dine at a never-ending buffet. They moved in and made themselves at home on farms and in granaries, enjoying the bounty of a resource boom. How do we know this? Digging around ancient sites in what is present-day Israel, archaeologists found mouse teeth in remains of grain stores dating back some eleven thousand years.

Mrs. Mus bred with a "let's make hay while the sun shines" approach. As she readily produces five to ten litters a year, with around six to eight youngsters a litter who reach sexual maturity in six weeks and start their own breeding program, it's not hard to imagine plague proportions and ruinous crop losses. It's not just what they eat that's the problem. It's what they spoil. One adult mouse eats about 3 grams of grain a day (that's about a teaspoon) but spoils from five to ten times more with its droppings and urine, bringing the total food losses up to 18 to 33 grams a day. Multiply that by 365 days, and in a year one mouse can potentially ruin anywhere from 6.5 to more than 12 kilograms (roughly 14 to 26 pounds) of grain.

When a free pest-control service arrived on the doorstep out of the blue, the farmers probably thought the gods were on their side. But it wasn't the gods. It was the easy pickings that lured the Near Eastern wildcat (*Felis silvestris lybica*), a solitary hunter, to step out of the desert and onto the farm, or at least its outskirts.

Over time, wildcats and farmers slipped into a comfortable and mutually beneficial working relationship. At some point, with the odd tasty tidbit or a friendly pat, farmers began encouraging wildcats to stick around after the harvest and use their pest-control prowess to protect the granaries year round. Some wildcats, ever open to a free lunch, embraced change. They settled down (in a feline sense) as farm cats and granary cats. They also found there were fringe benefits to enjoy when they stepped indoors—they discovered the human hearth was a pleasant place. They even sat on laps and very likely purred. They became tame cats or, as *sapiens* called them, "domestic cats."

No one knows exactly when or where all this took place, but it was certainly a fait accompli around four thousand years ago in Egypt. One of the earliest acknowledgments that felines were indispensable for pest control appears in the Rhind Papyrus:

> In seven houses there are seven cats. Each cat catches seven mice. If each mouse were to eat seven ears of corn and each ear of corn, if sown, were to produce seven gallons of grain, how many things are mentioned in total?

The 49 cats in those seven houses saved those seven farmers 16,807 gallons of grain.

Houses = 7
Cats = 7 x 7 (or 7^2) = 49
Mice caught = 7 x 7 x 7 (or 7^3) = 343
Ears of corn = 7 x 7 x 7 x 7 (or 7^4) = 2,401
Gallons of grain (if each ear of corn were sown) = 7 x 7 x 7 x 7 x 7 (or 7^5) = 16,807

Impressive though that is, it's not the answer the puzzle writer is looking for, which is the grand total of "things mentioned":

Grand total = 7 + 49 + 343 + 2,401 + 16,807 = 19,607

Incidentally . . .

Puzzled how corn got to Egypt from the Americas three thousand years before Columbus brought it back to Spain? It didn't. *Corn* is the old word for grain, "a small hard particle, a seed," going back to *grnom*, Indo-European for "worn down particle."

This is the only puzzle in the Rhind Papyrus in which felines save the day, but there are many others about grain and granaries. Grain built Egypt. Grain fed the masses—the thousands and thousands and thousands of laborers who built the pyramids and the dams and lakes that regulated the Nile, preventing floods and providing water in times of drought. And to make sure everyone got the grain they needed, Egypt needed managers who could not only manage but also compute.

The Rhind Papyrus was penned by the scribe Ahmes around 1550 BCE, though it may be older. It isn't ancient Egyptian Sudoku to puzzle away an idle afternoon. Its full title is *The Correct Method of Reckoning, for Grasping the Meaning of Things, and Knowing Everything—Obscurities and All Secrets*. Egypt was a world in which you had to be numerate "so that you may open treasuries and granaries, so that you may take delivery from one corn-bearing ship at the entrance to the granary, so that on feast days you may measure out the gods' offerings," so it's most likely this is simply a math practice book. In total, it has eighty-four practical problems (with solutions) that a young man on the way up must master to show potential employers he has the computing skills to handle a scribe's job. It wasn't cheap. At about sixteen feet (five meters) unrolled, a copy would set the purchaser back the equivalent of a small goat (two deben). It's the sort of investment ambitious parents might make to help set their son up in the world.

Incidentally . . .

Bemused by the "Rhind"? It's nothing to do with cheese. The papyrus is named after the Scottish antiquarian Alexander Henry Rhind, who picked it up quite possibly for a song in a market in 1858 and whose family bestowed it on the British Museum in 1864 after his death, and that's where it still is, behind glass in the Papyrus Room. Well, two parts of it are; the third is in the Brooklyn Museum in New York.

It's not surprising the call went out for farm cats and granary cats, with their exemplary pest-control track record, to sign on as mousers for the grain ships. Again, it's not known exactly when or where this took place first, but they took the plunge and became sea cats or seafurrers, as they prefer to be called.

Sapiens were possibly surprised at how readily their new shipmates found their sea legs. But felines have natural assets such as agility, balance, independence, patience, and perseverance that helped them take to life on the ocean waves like the proverbial duck to water. What's more, life at sea brought additional responsibilities that made the most of their superior hearing (which can pinpoint the source of a sound), sensitive nose (which can sniff out trouble spots), and superefficient eyes (which can see in very dim light). And with their inherent curiosity, seafurrers proved particularly invaluable on the watch—new sights, smells, or sounds, no matter how faint, merited immediate and undivided attention.

Mateship was the bonus. Seafarers and seafurrers provided each other with support and companionship during long absences from home. *Belgica's* Dr. Frederick Cook, commenting on their two-year voyage in Antarctica (1897–99), says Nansen, the ship's cat, was "the only speck of sentimental life within reach." Sailors and sea cats became shipmates.

Worse things happen at sea, they say, and for good reason. Along with reefs, rocks, storms, shipwrecks, and piracy, seafurrers faced a new enemy, what polar explorer Roald Amundsen called "the

The gun crew of HMAS *Sydney*'s port number 3 (P3) 6-inch gun, on the deck in front of the breech and gun shield

most repulsive of all creatures, and the worst vermin I know of": *Rattus rattus*—black rats or ship/ship's rats. They aren't necessarily black. They come in light fawn, chestnut brown with white patches, light gray, dark gray, and black. Whatever the color, they are formidable prey, ganging up and fighting in packs, and exceptionally dangerous when cornered. To make a kill, a rat will sacrifice its own life, no question. In 1858, Robert White Stevens, a longtime expert on ships and cargoes, doesn't hold back describing why the rat problem is so daunting:

Of all those [vermin] infesting ships, the rat is the most injurious, which arises from his great instinct, boldness, and natural qualifications. The inner portion of the four front teeth of rats is soft; the outer is composed of the strongest enamel; the continual growth of these teeth can only be checked by constant use. When one has been lost, the opposite tooth has been known to lengthen until it met the gum, which caused it to turn and ultimately to pass through the lip. It is this extraordinary growing property of the front teeth, coupled with an unconquerable thirst, which makes rats so formidable on board ship.

They certainly are omnivorous eating machines. They will devour pretty much anything and everything, chewing their way through the grain and whatever else is in the hold, and then through rations, ropes, boots, biscuits, sails, clothing, and the hard skin on the soles of sleeping sailors' feet.

One 12-ounce (350-gram) adult black rat eats about 4 ounces (115 grams) of food a day and spoils five to ten times more through its droppings and urine, adding up to a grand total of 1.5 to 2.75 pounds (690 to 1,265 grams) of spoiled grain a day. In a year one rat can potentially damage more than 1,000 pounds (462 kilograms) of food. It's no wonder shipping rules insisted a seafurrer be part of a ship's complement.

Incidentally . . .

We don't know when our first wildcat forebear was given a name, but it's likely it was soon after it stepped indoors and made itself at home on the farm as the resident pest controller and family pet. As for what names, it's reasonable to assume *sapiens* generally took the easy option with "Tabby" and "Ginger." There were certainly numerous pest controllers, shipmates, mascots, and pets on board called Tabby and Ginger, along with more imaginatively named seafurrers—Cleopatra, Queen Lil, Thomas Whiskers, Stowaway Jim, and Red Lead; and of course Simon, Trim, and Mrs. Chippy, who became celebs.

In the early years of the twentieth century, sailors sometimes bestowed the N-word—one of the most offensive racial slurs in the English language today—as a name on their intrepid seafurring shipmates. And, in fact, outrageous as it is today, *sapiens* often bestowed that name on any hapless pet or farm animal with black fur (or feathers) back then. That being said, there's no need to perpetuate past prejudices, and I have redacted instances of the name in my book (Incidents 18, 29, and 35).

MOUSERS AND MORE

"Tiger came aboard in Djibouti, French Somaliland. He was not invited, but just walked over the gangway of the cable-ship, of which I was Third Officer at the time, as if it belonged to him. He paid no attention to anyone in the way of greeting, but just got to work catching rats and eating them. No 'cat and mouse games' but serious business. We had rats—he wanted them, and he caught them and ate them. That suited us all right, so we allowed him to stay."

—*"Conquering Cat,"* Times *(London), March 9, 1960*

mouser: an animal that catches mice, especially a cat

ats have had a solid reputation as hunters in general and mousers in particular for thousands of years, long before the word *mouser* made its appearance in English as a definition in the fifteenth century in the first English-to-Latin dictionary, *Promptorium parvulorum*, or "storehouse for children": "Mowsare as a catte, *musceps*"—*musceps* meaning "mouser" in Latin.

Of course, cats weren't the only mousers. Any person whose day job was catching vermin might well be called Mouser, a respectable surname and sensible way to advertise expertise and promote services—Gerlacus Mus of Worms, 1257; Godwinus Mauser of Sangerhausen, 1268; and Robert Mouser of the Church of St. Andrew Holborn, London, 1575.

And then there were other animals. "Owls . . . are counted very good mousers," wrote Samuel Foote in his play *The Maid of Bath* (circa 1771), and the prowess of the long black snake really impressed John Lawson when he was exploring the American colonies: "He is the best Mouser that can be; for he leaves not one of that Vermine alive, where he comes," he reported in *A New Voyage to Carolina* (1709).

But owls and snakes aren't like cats. Nor are ferrets. Or the mongoose. While they may dispose of vermin effectively, they can't be house trained, and you may not want them around the house at all, which is why cats win the "mouser" crown hands down. "Chief Mouser to the Cabinet Office" is the title of the official resident cat at 10 Downing Street, the UK prime minister's

HQ, a paid position from June 3, 1929, when A. E. Banham at the treasury authorized the office keeper "to spend 1d [1 penny] a day from petty cash towards the maintenance of an efficient cat." The cat performed so well that they upped its allowance to 1s 6d (1 shilling and 6 pence) a week in April 1932.

Don't Forget the Cat

Il Consolato del Mare
(A Manual of Maritime Law: Consisting of a Treatise on Ships and Freight and a Treatise on Insurance)
Roccus (Francesco Rocco), 1809

" NOTE LVIII

If goods laden on board of a ship are devoured by rats, and the owners consequently suffer considerable damage, the master must repair the injury sustained by the owners, for he is considered in fault. But if the master kept cats on board, he is excused from that liability. "

ACCORDING TO BART

Roccus didn't write the manual of maritime law. Francis Celelles pulled it all together. An imaginative fifteenth-century early adopter, he was quick off the mark to spot an opportunity. He certainly wasn't afraid to roll up his sleeves and set to

work to do a job that needed to be done. We know this for a fact because it's reported that "Through charity alone, with much labour, frequent conferences, and advice with skillful aged persons, and recurrence to many authorities," Celelles took advantage of Johannes Gutenberg's movable type and printing press and published *Les costums marítimes de Barcelona universalment conegudes per Llibre del Consolat de mar* in Barcelona in 1494. (*Consolat* is Catalan for the Italian *consolato*, meaning consulate or consular court, the term for their maritime courts.)

Celelles didn't "write" the rules. He revised and updated a vast collection of existing rules from over the centuries that the judges in the maritime cities of the Mediterranean used to settle disputes at sea, of which there were many. It's not surprising the 1494 edition sold out, nor that numerous translations (including Roccus') followed.

Over time the rules were fine-tuned. It's not entirely fair to lumber the master with liability if he hadn't forgotten the ship's cat at all and had in fact signed on a top-notch pest-controlling seafurrer who sadly was washed overboard in a horrific storm at sea while stalking a rat. So, Note LVIII version two adds:

If the ship has had cats on board in the place where she was loaded, and after she has sailed away the said cats have died, and the rats have damaged the goods, if the managing owner of the ship shall buy cats and put them on board as soon as they arrive at a place where they can find them, he is not bound to make good the said losses, for they have not happened through his default.

Most shipmasters didn't need a rules book to tell them what to do. It was common sense to add a seafurrer or two to the crew to handle pest control, and common practice on merchant ships. The charter party of the *Anne of Hull* carried "a doge and a cat with all other necessaryes" on her voyage to the Isle of Man in 1532, according to English Admiralty records.

Incidentally . . .

Good mousers bring to their work what Robert Pirsig called "self-reliance and old-fashioned gumption" in his bestselling *Zen and the Art of Motorcycle Maintenance*. They also enhance their hit rate with seven highly effective habits.

Good mousers:

- Practice: They hone their skills.
- Persevere: If at first they don't succeed, they try again.
- Are patient: They know it's a waiting game, not a race.
- Plan: They study moves and become familiar with the lay of the land.
- Are flexible: They keep fit and on top of their game.
- Maintain life balance: They avoid burnout. They don't overdo it.
- Keep a healthy sense of proportion: They don't dwell on the ones that got away.

South Sea Adventures

The Observations of Sir Richard Hawkins, Knt,
in His Voyage into the South Sea in the Year 1593

" Heere we made also a survay of our victuals; and opening certaine barrels of oaten meale, wee found a great part of some of them, as also of our pipes and fatts [vats] of bread, eaten and consumed by the ratts; doubtlesse, a fift [fifth] part of my company did not eate so much these devoured, as wee found dayly in comming to spend any of our provisions.

When I came to the sea, it was not suspected that I had a ratt in my shippe; but with the bread in caske, which we transported out of the *Hawke*, and the going to and againe of our boates unto our prise, though wee had divers catts and used other preventions, in a small time they multiplyed in such a maner as is incredible. It is one of the generall calamities of all long voyages, and would bee carefully prevented as much as may bee. For besides that which they consume of the best victuals,

they eate the sayles; and neither packe nor chest is free from their surprises. I have knowne them to make a hole in a pipe of water, and saying the pumpe, have put all in feare, doubting least some leake had beene sprung upon the ship.

Moreover, I have heard credible persons report, that shippes have beene put in danger by them to be sunke, by a hole made in the bulge. "

# ACCORDING TO BART

What with scurvy's scourge, shipwreck, and piracy, long-distance voyaging took a fair bit of courage and optimism. But not suspecting "a ratt in my shippe" was more than optimism—it was the triumph of hope over experience. There were always rats on ships, and they always got into the provisions and more besides. However, having a "hole made in the bulge" is possibly a bit of a stretch. If there's any truth in the rumor that rats leave a sinking ship, why would they hole the hull to prove the point?

Hawkins was a seafaring man with a grand plan. Coming from a renowned family of "sea dogs," he may well have felt he had something to prove when he decided to make a voyage by way of the Strait of Magellan and the South Sea

> to make a perfect discovery of all those parts where I should arrive, as well knowne as unknowne, with their longitudes, and latitudes; the lying of their coasts; their head-lands; their ports, and bayes; their cities, townes, and peoplings; their manner of government; with the commodities which the countries yeelded, and of which they have want, and are in necessitie.

Which all sounds very worthy (and wordy), but was code for plundering treasure-laden Spanish galleons plying the Pacific. It was a family thing. His dad, Admiral Sir John Hawkins, had dabbled in privateering (and a bit of slave trading), as had his globe-circumnavigating cousin Sir Francis Drake.

Setting sail in June 1593, Hawkins made his way through the straits into the South Sea and headed north, taking a number of prizes before being overpowered by the Spanish and taken prisoner. He never set foot in the East. But he did eventually get home. He was ransomed in 1602 for the £3,000 (around £345,000, or $454,584, in today's money) left him by his dad and reluctantly paid out by his stepmother.

Ferdinand Magellan had pushed south for a westward passage to the East and paved the way for such South Sea adventures. He was convinced that by sailing down the Patagonian coast farther than anyone had been before he would find the mystery passage around the Americas to the "South Sea" (Pacific Ocean), which Vasco Núñez de Balboa had seen on September 25, 1513, when he crossed the Isthmus of Panama. And he was right, reported Antonio Pigafetta:

> After going and taking the course to the fifty-second degree of the said Antarctic sky, on the day of the Eleven Thousand Virgins [October 21], we found, by a miracle, a strait which we called the Cape of the Eleven Thousand Virgins [now Cabo Virgenes], this strait is a hundred and ten leagues long, which are four hundred and forty miles, and almost as wide as less than half a league, and it issues in another sea, which is called the peaceful sea.

Magellan took thirty-eight days to find his way through the narrow passage "surrounded by very great and high mountains covered with snow," including a tasty stopover at the River of Sardines. He headed north and by good fortune found the trade winds that blew him to the Philippines. But he never got home to enjoy the rewards of his initiative to push south for a westward passage to the East—he was killed in a skirmish on Cebu.

He may be the one with his name in the history books, but Magellan wasn't the first South Sea explorer—not by a long shot. The forebears of the people he ran into in the Philippines knew all about trade winds and navigating by the stars. They packed their canoes with their pigs, dogs, and chickens and began a great migration about four thousand years ago and settled, traded, and planted gardens island by island. *Rattus exulans* (the Polynesian rat) joined them for the ride and the cooking pot. But there were no seafurrers on board, making Magellan's able-bodied sea cats likely the first to cross the Pacific.

Long before Magellan rounded Cabo Deseado, Polynesian voyagers had made their way to South America and discovered the delights of the sweet potato. They loved this orange-fleshed veg so much, they pretty much worshipped it. When the Maori packed their canoes for the Great Migration to Aotearoa (New Zealand), they took their sweet potatoes with them and planted them in their gardens, and that's where Captain James Cook spotted them growing in 1769:

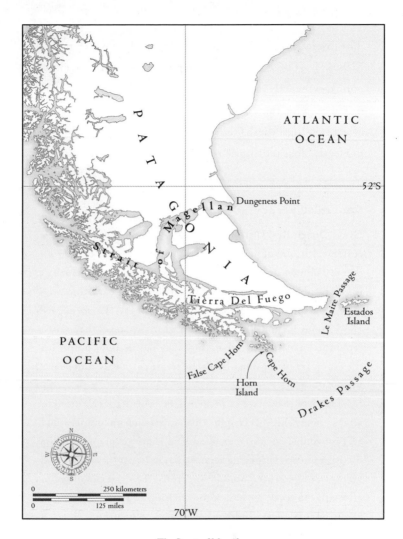

The Strait of Magellan

MOUSERS AND MORE

The Sweet potatoes are set out in distinct little mole-hills. . . . The Arum [taro] is planted in little circular concaves, exactly in the manner our Gard'ners plant melons. . . . The Yams are planted in like manner with the sweet potatoes: these Cultivated spots are enclosed with a perfectly close pailing of reeds about twenty inches high.

Incidentally . . .

Good Queen Bess (Elizabeth I) was very fond of boosting her coffers with a bit of bounty. That's why she granted Hawkins a commission (as she had with other Elizabethan sea dogs such as his dad and his cousin) "to attempt, with a ship, bark, and pinnace, an expedition against Philip II of Spain." The deal gave Hawkins Junior and his backers the right to whatever they looted from the Spanish (of course, they also had to divvy it up with the crew), reserving one fifth of the treasure, jewels, and pearls for the queen.

Think of privateers as government contractors licensed to attack enemy ships. If caught, they were generally imprisoned and ransomed by family or friends or their government. The Spanish found ransoming a handy way to boost the coffers and recover dungeon accommodation costs—the dead can't pay up, after all. However, without a commission or letter of marque, captured privateers would be considered to be pirates (it was a fine line at times) and strung up on a handy headland.

Survivor

A Cruising Voyage Round the World
Captain Woodes Rogers, 1712

" He [Alexander Selkirk] had with him his Clothes and Bedding, with a Firelock, some Powder, Bullets, and Tobacco, a Hatchet, a Knife, a Kettle, a Bible, some practical Pieces, and his Mathematical Instruments and Books. He diverted and provided for himself as well as he could; but for the first eight months had much ado to bear up against Melancholy, and The terror of being left alone in such a desolate place. He built two Hutts with Piemento Trees, cover'd them with long Grass, and lin'd them with the Skins of Goats, which he kill'd with his own Gun as he wanted, so long as his Powder lasted, which was but a pound; and that being near spent, he got Fire by rubbing two sticks of Piemento Wood together on his knee. . . .

After he had conquer'd his Melancholy, he diverted himself sometimes by cutting his Name on the Trees, and of the Time of his being left and Continuance there. He was at first much pester'd with Cats and Rats, that had bred in great numbers from some of each Species which had got ashore from Ships that put in there to wood and water. The Rats gnaw'd his Feet and Clothes while asleep, which oblig'd him to cherish the Cats with his Goats-flesh; by which many of them became so tame, that they would lie about him in hundreds, and soon deliver'd him from the Rats. He likewise tam'd some Kids, and to divert himself would now and then sing and dance with them and his Cats: so that by the Care of Providence and Vigour of his Youth, being now but about 30 years old, he came at last to conquer all the Inconveniences of his Solitude, and to be very easy.

ACCORDING TO BART

Captain Woodes Rogers wasn't just passing by. Since its discovery in 1574, the Juan Fernández archipelago (just off the coast of Chile) was a regular pit stop for ships plying the Pacific to stock up with wood, water, greens, goat meat, and fish. It had also been home to a couple of abandoned attempts at settlement by the Spanish (they brought goats and pigs, and later dogs to keep the goats down) and numerous castaways and

deserters. Selkirk had taken shore leave to escape, he told journalist Richard Steele when back in London, "from a leaky Vessel, with the Captain of which he had had an irreconcilable difference; and he chose rather to take his Fate in this place, than in a crazy Vessel, under a disagreeable Commander." He didn't expect to be stuck there for four years and four months. He could possibly have left earlier, but with a background in privateering, he thought discretion the better part of valor and made himself scarce when Spanish ships dropped anchor in the bay.

As for the cats that "deliver'd him from the Rats," they were likely descendants of Spanish seafurrers who had stepped ashore to stretch their legs and missed the boat. Or perhaps, like Selkirk, they had decided jumping ship was preferable to going down with it. Selkirk was not only savvy; he was possibly psychic. The ship he jumped, the *Cinque Ports*, leaked so heavily that the crew took to the rafts after leaving Juan Fernández and headed for the coast of South America. The eighteen survivors (including the captain) were picked up by the Spanish and put in prison—the Spanish and English were at war again, this time the War of the Spanish Succession, 1701–14.

The cats on the island, in any case, certainly had a full-time job with the robust rat population. From all accounts, everyone seemed to dine rather better living off the fat of the land on the island than they ever did on board. Numerous dietary delights were on the menu because the nine men that buccaneer Edward Davis left behind in 1687 had planted corn and vegetables and hunted goats, seals, and mutton birds before being rescued.

In addition, "Fish, particularly Snappers and Rock-fish, are so plentiful, that two Men in an hours time will take with Hook and Line, as many as will serve 100 Men," wrote William Dampier. Selkirk was a fussy eater, but even he discovered the delights of "Crawfish." Woodes Rogers wrote:

He might have had Fish enough, but could not eat 'em for want of Salt, because they occasion'd a Looseness; except Crawfish, which are there as large as our Lobsters, and very good: These he sometimes boil'd, and at other times broil'd, as he did his Goats Flesh, of which he made very good Broth, for they are not so rank as ours: he kept an Account of 500 that he kill'd while there, and caught as many more, which he mark'd on the Ear and let go.

Juan Fernández is no longer for pit stops or castaways. The archipelago has a new identity—Juan Fernández National Park—and the island on which Selkirk was marooned a new name: Robinson Crusoe Island. Visitors can fly in, tuck into the clawless Juan Fernández lobster, go adventuring, and fly out, all in a matter of days.

Incidentally . . .

Did Selkirk's story inspire Daniel Defoe's *Robinson Crusoe*? Possibly. But there were other Juan Fernández survivor stories doing the rounds at the time, such as Dampier's account of the resourceful "Moskito Indian" left there in 1681:

> This Indian lived here alone above three years, and altho' he was several times sought after by the *Spaniards*,

---

who knew he was left on the Island, yet they could never find him. He was in the Woods, hunting for Goats, when Capt. *Watlin* drew off his Men, and the Ship was under sail before he came back to shore. He had with him his Gun and a Knife, with a small Horn of Powder, and a few Shot; which being spent, he contrived a way by notching his Knife, to saw the Barrel of his Gun into small Pieces, wherewith he made Harpoons, Lances, Hooks and a long Knife; heating the pieces first in the fire, which he struck with his Gunflint, and a piece of the Barrel of his Gun, which he hardned; having learnt to do that among the *English*. The hot pieces of Iron he would hammer out and bend as he pleased with Stones, and saw them with his jagged Knife, or grind them to an Edge by long labour, and harden them to a good temper as there was occasion. All this may seem strange to those that are not acquainted with the sagacity of the *Indians*; but it is no more than these *Moskito* Men are accustomed to in their own Country, where they make their own Fishing and striking Instruments, without either Forge or Anvil; tho' they spend a great deal of time about them.

Sailing into History

The *Endeavour* Journal of Joseph Banks, 1768–1771
Edited by J. C. Beaglehole

> [1768—September] 28. Wind rather slackend; three birds were today about the ship, a swallow, to all appearance the same as our European one, and two motacillas, about night fall one of the latter was taken; about 11 a shoal of Porpoises came about the ship, and the fisgig was soon thrown into one of them but would not hold.
>
> 29. This morn calm; employd in drawing and describing the bird taken yesterday, calld it Motacilla avida; while the drawing was in hand it became very familiar, so much so that we had a brace made for it in hope to keep it alive; as flies were in amazing abundance onboard the ship we had no fear of plentiful supply of provision.

30. This Morn at day break made the Island of Bonavista, one of the Cape Verde Islands: Mr Buchan employd in taking views of the land; Mr Parkinson busy in finishing the sketches made of the shark yesterday.

This Evening the other Motacilla avida was brought to us, it differd scarce at all from the first taken, except that it was something larger; his head however gave us some good, by supplying us with near twenty specimens of ticks, which differd but little from the acarus vicinus Linn; it was however described and calld Motacilla.

[October] 21. Trade continues. Today the cat killd our bird M. Avida who had lived with us ever since the 29th of Septr intirely on the flies which he caught for himself; he was hearty and in high health so that probably he might have livd a great while longer had fate been more kind.

ACCORDING TO BART

Joe should have been more careful about letting the perky little wagtail he was so fond of fly around the cabin. He would know (a) the ship was overrun with rats and (b) Cook was always recruiting seafurrers to deal with the problem. The presence of rats and able-bodied sea cats would have been hard to miss on a

small Whitby collier converted for the world's first major scientific venture at sea—to calculate the distance between the earth and the sun by measuring Venus (it would look like a little black disk from planet Earth) transiting the sun.

That was the Royal Society of London's mission, but not Joe's. He was an ambitious young man of considerable wealth, with big plans and a large retinue (naturalists Daniel Solander and H. D. Spöring; landscape and natural history artists Alexander Buchan and Sydney Parkinson; assistants James Roberts and Peter Briscoe; and his two servants Thomas Richmond and George Dorlton).

When Joe set sail for the South Seas, collector John Ellis reported to Carl Linnaeus that the £10,000 (around £550,000, or $724,699, in today's money) of equipment he took with him included his

fine Library of Natural History . . . all sorts of machines for catching and preserving insects; all kinds of nets, trawls, drags and hooks for coral fishing . . . a curious contrivance of a telescope, by which, put into the water, you can see the bottom to a great depth, where it is clear . . . many cases of bottles with ground stoppers, of several sizes, to preserve animals in spirits . . . several sorts of salts to surround the seeds; and wax, both beeswax and that of *Myrica*.

Joe's plan was to be the first naturalist to go plant hunting and species seeking in the South Seas.

He was. Three years later he and Solander arrived home with a massive collection of about thirty thousand plants, shells, insects, and animals representing some three thousand species, of which thirteen hundred were wholly new to Europe's scientists. Even if only half that number were animals or insects, that's still a considerable number of living things meeting their end in little bottles of spirits compared with one small *Motacilla* meeting its "fate" because someone left the door open. Joe also introduced the stuffed kangaroo to the world.

Incidentally . . .

Joe Banks was on the spot when the Union Jack was hoisted and Australia (well, its east coast, called New South Wales back then) was added to the British Empire. What's long forgotten is that he was also once known as the Father of Australia. As David Hunt wrote in his unauthorized history of Australia, *Girt*:

> It was Banks who first recommended that the British establish a penal colony at Botany Bay. It was Banks who influenced early British thinking on relations with Aboriginal people and advised the Crown on all matters New South Welsh during the first decades of settlement. It was Banks who instructed Matthew Flinders to circumnavigate Australia to put beyond doubt that it was a single continent. It was Banks who stole merinos from the Spanish, allowing generations of Australians to ride on the sheep's back. And it was Banks who got the mutiny-prone William Bligh into both breadfruit and governorship, indirectly contributing to the only military coup in Australian history. Banks' role in shaping Australia was so neglected over the years that he wasn't recognised on an Australian stamp until 1970, and then he was only a background figure. Banks wasn't even the first botanist to be licked and stuffed into an Australian post box, this honour falling to Sir Ferdinand Jakob Heinrich von Mueller in 1948 for his services to the macadamia nut.

INCIDENT 5

Beating Scurvy's Scourge

A Journal of Captain Cook's Last Voyage to the Pacific Ocean, on Discovery; Performed in the Years 1776, 1777, 1778, 1779
John Rickman, 1781

" [Table Bay, Cape of Good Hope]

On the 11th [October 1776], came to and anchored in six fathom water, where, to our great joy, we found the Resolution. . . .

Captain Cook, with the principal officers and gentlemen belonging to the ship, came on board to bid us welcome. By them we learnt that they had been at the Cape near three weeks. . . .

What remained for Captain Cook to do when we arrived, was chiefly to purchase live cattle for presents to Arees [i.e., Polynesian chiefs] in the South Seas; likewise live stock for the ships use; these are always the last things provided, because it is found necessary to shorten, as much as possible, their continuance on board. . . .

Among the cattle purchased, were four horses and mares of a delicate breed, for Omai [the Polynesian being returned to Tahiti]; several bulls and cows of the buffaloe kind, as more suitable to the tropical climates than any brought from Europe; likewise some African rams and ewes; some dogs too were purchased; cats we had plenty on board, and of goats Captain Cook purchased numbers of both sexes.

Stored with these, the Resolution resembled the Ark, in which all the animals that were to stock the little world to which he was bound were collected; and with their provender, they occupied no small part of the ship's stowage. "

ACCORDING TO BART

The *Resolution* may have had plenty of able-bodied sea cats back in Cape Town, but all that changed at Moorea, according to Cook. "The Ship being a good [deal] pestered with rats, I hauled her within thirty yards of the Shore, being as near as the depth of water would allow." Midshipman William Charlton "got a Hawser [a large rope] out of the Ballast Port with some Spars lash't upon it with a desire to get some of the Rats out of the Ship, we having a Great Number of them on board." The idea behind hawsering is that the rats would, Pied Piper–like, take to the

tightrope and head for the shore. Obviously some did, maybe lots did. The locals quite reasonably responded to having ships' rats offloaded on their island with a spot of cat snatching for pest control, to send Captain Cook a clear "don't make your solution our problem" message. That's why the shipboard pest-control resources were depleted, though the locals did eventually return a couple of seafurrers.

While Cook came to an untimely end and the expedition didn't discover a Northwest Passage around North America, they did notch up some achievements. They charted large tracts of the Pacific and Arctic coasts of North America and Russia, and no case of scurvy was reported. At a time when a long sea trip could be a death sentence, Cook's "eat your greens" diet plan (which meant large amounts of "Sour Krout") kept his crew free from scurvy's scourge. And that became his legacy, at least for his men, as the musical testimonial that follows shows.

Cook wasn't the only fruit and veg preacher sailing the high seas, but he was the standout in getting his men to eat their greens. He was a prodigious stocker-upper of fresh supplies on every possible occasion. And he was an absolute stickler: Everyone had to eat their greens. He didn't force-feed; he used psychology. He served Sour Kraut on *Endeavour* to the officers, and let the men take it or leave it. They took it—as soon as seamen see "their Superiors set a Value upon it, it becomes the finest stuff in the World," he revealed in his *Endeavour* journal (1768–71).

Captain Cook's men certainly knew he saved their lives. Able Seaman Thomas Perry from HMS *Resolution* composed a celebratory song with this verse:

We were all hearty seamen no cold did we fear
And we have from all sickness entirely kept clear
Thanks be to the Captain he has proved so good
Amongst all the Islands to give us fresh food.

Incidentally . . .

Seafurrers don't need to "eat their greens," let alone dose up on Sour Kraut. Like most other mammals except guinea pigs, some bats, and most primates (*sapiens* included), felines make their own vitamin C, giving them a considerable nutritional advantage on long voyages over their scurvy-prone shipmates.

Naming Rights

A Voyage of Discovery and Research in the Southern and Antarctic Regions, During the Years 1839–43
Captain Sir James Clark Ross, 1847

" Feb. 21 [1842]: The southerly gale continued to blow with violence during the whole of the next day, and with the thermometer at 19° [Fahrenheit] the waves, which broke over the ships, froze as they fell on the decks and rigging; by this means a heavy weight of ice accumulated about the hull and ropes which kept the crew constantly employed with axes, breaking it away; and from their exposure to the inclemency of the weather, several of them suffered severely. A remarkable circumstance occurred on board the Terror during this storm, which may help to convey a better idea of the intensity of the cold we experienced than the mere reference to the state of the thermometer. Whilst her people were engaged chopping away the thick coat of ice from her bows, which had been formed by the freezing of a portion of each wave that she plunged into, a small fish was found in the mass; it must have been dashed against the ship, and instantly frozen fast. It was carefully removed for the purpose of preservation, a sketch of it made, and its dimensions taken by Dr. Robertson, but it was unfortunately seized upon and devoured by a cat. Dr. Richardson observes [in *Zoology of the Voyage*], 'that the sketch is not sufficiently detailed to show either the number or nature of the gill and fin rays, or whether the skin was scaly or not, so that even the order to which the fish belongs is uncertain, and we have introduced a copy of the design, merely to preserve a memorial of what appears to be a novel form, discovered under such peculiar circumstances.' It was rather more than six inches in length. "

ACCORDING TO BART

Fish makes a nice change, and it would be easy to argue that eating it was a better outcome all round than pickling it to preserve, measure, and then put it in a museum drawer to gather dust.

Ross is rather relaxed about all this, and his would have been a good ship to serve on. After all, he's the man who rammed his ships through the pack ice into the open water beyond and, he claimed, "discovered a land of so extensive a coastline and attaining such an altitude as to justify the appellation of a Great New

Southern Continent." All aboard were awestruck. And according to the dipping needles, they were also close to finding what they were looking for: the magnetic south pole. That's why there are lots of "Rosses" in Antarctica—Ross Sea, Ross Ice Shelf, Ross Island, Ross Dependency—James Clark Ross got there first.

Being first on the scene gives you naming rights. It's not (entirely) about ego; places need names so you can put them on a map and find them again. Ross named the Admiralty Range after his sponsors (the admiralty), Cape Adare after a friend, Victoria Land after the queen, Mount Erebus (an active volcano rising 12,448 feet/3,794 meters skyward) after his ship, and Mount Terror (a smaller extinct

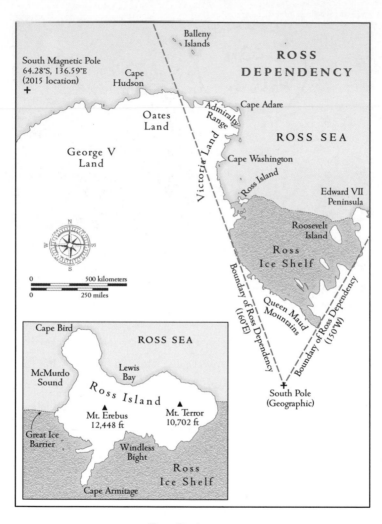

"Rosses" in Antarctica

volcano rising to 10,702 feet/3,262 meters) after the other ship in the expedition. He called the wall of ice rising 160 feet (50 meters) out of the sea and extending "as far to the east and west as the eye could discern" (thus putting an end to sailing farther south) the Great Ice Barrier, and the sea where he met the barrier McMurdo Sound, after the first lieutenant on the *Terror*. As for the dear departed fish, it's nameless. No one knows what it was. But as there was none left over, it was obviously tasty.

Ross was a polar pro. Discovering Antarctica was no lucky break. For seventeen of the previous twenty years, he'd been on Arctic expeditions, and had located the north magnetic pole (1831). "Be prepared" was his motto. He knew what lay ahead. He did his homework, stocked up for three years with copious quantities of food, including scurvy-beating vegetable soup, pickled cabbage, and carrots, and packed plenty of ice saws, some portable forges, warm winter kit for the crew, a small flock of sheep, and seafurrers (note the reference to "a" cat, not "the" cat) for pest control. "Few people of the present day are capable of rightly appreciating this heroic deed, this brilliant proof of human courage and energy," reckoned explorer Roald Amundsen, no novice himself in polar parts:

With two ponderous craft—regular "tubs" according to our ideas—these men sailed right into the heart of the pack, which all previous explorers had regarded as certain death. . . . These men were heroes—heroes in the highest sense of the word.

Incidentally . . .

"The cat is fain the fish to eat, but hath no will to wet her feet" is a saying that goes way back into the proverbial mists—*Cat lufat visch, ac he nele his feth wete* in Middle English, from the Latin *Catus amat piscem, sed non vult tangere flumen*. However, why cats? People eat plenty of fish without ever dangling a line, let alone getting their "paws" wet or going anywhere near water. They also overfish, but that's another story. Fishing cats (*Prionailurus viverrinus*) aren't afraid to get their (partially webbed) paws wet. And they do from time to time eat fish. But they are just as partial to frogs, waterfowl, mollusks, and crayfish, along with rats, mice, insects, and snakes.

Raw fish isn't actually ideal fare for felines despite proverbial wisdom. It contains thiaminase, an enzyme that breaks down thiamin (an essential water-soluble B vitamin) and can lead to a "head-messing" thiamin deficiency, beriberi, and an untimely end. Prevention is better than cure. Cooking kills thiaminase.

Collectomania

A Landlubber's Log of His Voyage Around Cape Horn
Morton MacMichael III, 1883

" July 25 [1879].—During the morning passed through a large fleet of nautilus, those renowned little creatures of the jelly-fish species, that spread their tiny film-like sails in delicate shades of pink and blue, and cruise about over the waves, sometimes alone or in little groups, and again, as I first saw them, in vast numbers. The sunlight playing on the thousands of rising and falling sails made a very pretty picture. We were slopping along at a lazy pace when we overtook the fleet, which was running before a gentle breeze just strong enough to suit the sailing qualities of its tiny craft, and after scoring several misses in my attempts to catch one, I succeeded at last in slipping a bucket directly beneath a beauty and hauled it aboard without disturbing it in the slightest degree. Placing the bucket on deck, I went forward to call the carpenter and show him my prize. As we started aft we saw one of the ship's cats approach the bucket and proceed to investigate the nautilus, doubtless attracted by its fishy odor, and before we could interfere puss had captured the prize, and was scampering away with it. Another name common to the nautilus is that of Portuguese men-of-war, and this specimen promptly gave evidence of its warlike nature by stinging the cat before she had carried it across the deck, pussy dropping it with a terrified yowl, and vanishing into her sanctum, the galley, as though a dozen dogs were at her heels. During the rest of the day she sat in a corner, uttering plaintive meyows, and alternately rubbing her cheeks on the deck or scraping her swollen tongue with one of her front paws. . . .

August 13. . . . the most wonderful thing about the ship was the assortment of cats they had on board. There were actually twenty-eight live felines of every color and size, from a jet black Tom as big as a cat can grow to a little white kitten with its eyes still shut, the sole survivor of a recent lot, its brothers and sisters having been tossed overboard. Most of these cats were kept down between decks, and lived on rats, of which there were great numbers. This, in fact, was the reason for keeping so many, and it was an experiment of the captain's, the rodents having heretofore damaged a great deal of cargo.

August 22.—We were again surrounded by the Cape pigeons. . . . The afternoon being nearly calm I baited a small fish-hook with pork, and scattered some small bits about in the water. The pigeons promptly ate all the loose bits, and then turned their attention to the piece on the hook. A great many picked at it, but for an hour I couldn't hook one. At last, however, one unlucky chap got the barb fastened in his bill, and was hauled on board struggling bravely. Being unfit to eat I let it go again, after shutting it up for awhile in the cabin along with our youngest cat. Puss has been almost crazy since the birds came around, sitting up on the rail at the risk of falling overboard, and following them in their flight with her eyes for an hour at a time, and occasionally uttering a dismal 'meyow.' She also sharpened her claws very often, which led us to think she would tackle a bird with great vigor. But when pussy was brought face to face with our pigeon she weakened. For a while she only sat and looked at it sitting on the floor, then she went a little closer, when the bird hit her a slap right across the face with its wing. That finished the encounter, for the kitten retired under the sofa, from which retreat she could not be coaxed. 99

 ## ACCORDING TO BART

Dietary variety is important for good health, so it's no wonder "puss" headed for the "prize" if she had been living off rats for weeks. She certainly would not have understood the need to simply collect stuff. Seafurrers travel light.

Sapiens don't. They collect things. Sir Joseph Banks holds the single-voyage collecting world record, coming in at thirty thousand plants, shells, insects, and animals preserved in spirits, salts, or wax (*Endeavour*, 1769–72). Charles Darwin (*Beagle*, 1831–36) was no slouch, amassing a vast collection including nearly five hundred bird skins, whole birds preserved in spirits, various bird parts, and a small number of nests and eggs. What happened to all this stuff? A fair bit of dust gathering and crumbling to dust in drawers on the downside. On the upside, a lifetime of sorting and systematic labeling following the Linnaean system, which led to game-changing ideas about who we are, where we come from, and how we fit into the great scheme of things with the publication of Darwin's *On the Origin of Species* (November 24, 1859).

Carl Linnaeus was no globe-trotting collector; he was the man with the plan that gave collectors like Banks and Darwin an effective way of organizing their collections with his system of families, genera, and so forth. Observing the lower jawbone of a horse at the side of a road he was traveling in Lapland was apparently his "road to Damascus" moment. "If I only knew how many teeth and of what kind every animal had, how many teats and where they were placed, I should perhaps be able to work out a perfectly natural system for the arrangement of all quadrupeds," it's widely reported he thought to himself, though he doesn't seem to have written it down anywhere. However, it makes a nice story.

Young Morton MacMichael III, entertaining himself on a long sea voyage before the days when cruise directors came up with alternative plans to fill the time, was also a collector—Linnaeus would probably put him in the "idle curiosity, pick it up and drop it" category. The Portuguese man-of-war he hauled aboard in a bucket didn't live to tell the tale, but the Cape pigeon caught on a small fishhook possibly did. It was certainly a feisty bird with the good fortune of being labeled unfit to eat.

The Portuguese man-of-war is also unfit to eat—there's not much of it to eat, as it's 95 percent water. MacMichael called it a nautilus, but it's not. Nor is it remotely related to either the chambered nautilus, with its series of gas-filled chambers and an external shell lined with mother-of-pearl, or the paper nautilus (or argonaut), with its webbed, sail-like arms, the female of which secretes a thin, coiled papery shell to protect eggs. Nor, despite being boneless and drifting along with the crowd, is it a jellyfish, though it's distantly related. It isn't one organism but a whole colony of specialist organisms ("polyps" or "zooids" in tech speak) that have successfully teamed up since they can't survive on their own. On top is the harmless gas-filled bladder floating above the water that gives the Portuguese man-of-war its name; the sting, as is so often the case, is in the tail—the tentacles are thirty-three feet (ten meters) long, with venom-filled nematocysts (stinging cells) for paralyzing and killing prey such as fish or plankton. Being made up mostly of water, it's not a collector's item, whereas any sort of pearly shelled nautilus long has been and still is—just check out eBay.

Track *nautilus* back and you'll find it's ancient Greek for "sailor"— *nautilos*. Google it and you'll discover it's a popular name for everything from restaurants by the sea to weight-training machines in gyms far from the sea (though they probably have them on cruise ships). It's also the name for four rather famous submarines:

- Robert Fulton's submersible funded by Napoleon (1800)
- Captain Nemo's *Nautilus*, in Jules Verne's *Twenty Thousand Leagues Under the Sea* (1870)
- Andrew Campbell and James Ash's electric-powered submarine (1886)

• USS *Nautilus*, the world's first nuclear-powered vessel (1954).

Incidentally . . .

The opening of the Panama Canal was still thirty-five years away when MacMichael went a-voyaging, so the options for sailing from an Atlantic coast port to a Pacific coast port were going through the Strait of Magellan or rounding Cape Horn (see map on page 23). As far as we know, the first sailors who rounded the Horn were Jacques Le Maire and Willem Corneliszoon Schouten. They went looking for the fabled southernmost continent. They didn't tick that box, but they discovered something rather more useful on January 29, 1616:

> Wee saw land againe lying north west and north north-west from us, which was the land that lay South from the straights of Magellan which reacheth Southward, all high hillie lande covered over with snow, ending with a sharpe point which wee called Kaap Hoorn [Cape Horne]. . . .

Despite its storms, waves, icebergs, and deserved reputation as the graveyard of ships, sailors, and seafurrers, rounding the Horn became the preferred route from Atlantic to Pacific for sailing ships. Steam ships from the nineteenth century generally opted for the more protected waters of the Strait of Magellan until the Panama Canal opened in 1914.

Flying Cephalopods

"Dr. Clarke's Fish Story"
San Francisco Call, *August 9, 1904*

" The liner Ventura on her outward voyage, when between
this port and Honolulu, passed through a shower of squid,
which delighted the ship's cat and puzzled everybody else.
Dr. Clarke, the liner's surgeon, vouches for the story, and
volunteers the information that the wingless, finless, pis-
catorial curiosities must have been lifted from the ocean in
a waterspout and traveled to the Ventura's deck in a shower
of rain. In proof of his story he has two of the fish preserved in a bottle.

Professor J. E. Deuriden of Ann Arbor University,
who was a passenger, corroborated Surgeon Clarke's
diagnosis as to the family the fish represented. They can
neither jump nor fly, he says, and as the sea was smooth,
their presence on deck was a mystery. Then Dr. Clarke
volunteered the waterspout theory.

It was the ship's cat that discovered the squid. She was on deck for an early morning constitutional. Suddenly from the sky came a mess of fresh fish, all alive. The first squid the cat tackled squirted an ink-like fluid in the feline's face, and for a while this fountain-pen feature of the heaven-sent meal mystified puss.

When discovered by a sailor the cat had got away with all but half a dozen of the squid. Her face was stained with the dark-hued fluid with which each squid was plentifully supplied, but she was having the feast of her life, and, anyway, had learned early in life how to wash herself.

ACCORDING TO BART

Dr. Clarke's home-delivery theory is a possibility. It can rain fish after a waterspout. The whip-fast winds suck them up out of the water and into the cloud, sometimes carrying them miles before they fall to back to sea or crash on a passing deck. But that's not the most likely explanation for the *Ventura*'s shower of squid.

As waterspouts are essentially tornadoes at sea, you would expect those on board to be commenting on such an alarming meteorological event, even if it were merely a fair-weather waterspout, which develops on the surface of the water on a seemingly calm day and works its way upward, rather than a serious marine hazard—a downward-developing tornadic waterspout with full-on thunder, lightning, high winds, and hail.

The smart money is on flying cephalopods here. No one knows why some squid fly, but they may be fleeing predators, an entirely plausible reason to change direction and take off. They don't have to do anything special. They stick to their swimming technique, squirting a high-pressure jet of water out of their mantles and shooting out of the water. Since a picture is worth a thousand words, a graphic showing how they do it is warranted.

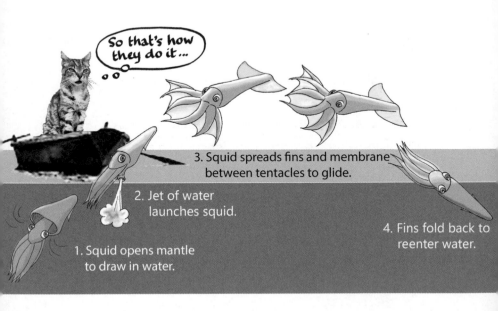

So that's how they do it ...

3. Squid spreads fins and membrane between tentacles to glide.

2. Jet of water launches squid.

4. Fins fold back to reenter water.

1. Squid opens mantle to draw in water.

While flying may be common for some squid, catching them in the act is rare because it all happens so fast. How fast? Olympic-medal fast for the Japanese flying squid, which can do the 30-meter dash in three seconds. To put some numbers on that: Usain Bolt, who won gold in London in 2012 by zipping along at 10.31 meters per second, would come in a poor second behind their 11.2 meters per second. However, the seafurrer's cousin the cheetah would have easily lapped them, coming in at 29 meters per second.

As for landings: not always happy. Flying squid obviously intend to drop back into the briny, but sadly (or fortunately, depending on your standpoint) some occasionally thump down on the deck of a ship where an altogether other fate awaits. All are edible.

Incidentally . . .

Currently around six species of cephalopods are known to fly. Some fly solo, while others burst from the water as a squadron. Some spread out their fins and arms in a radial pattern; others keep their arms folded tightly while rapidly flapping their fins. A few seem to keep jetting water while flying. Here's a not-definitive "you've been spotted" or "we've caught you on camera" list:

- *Dosidicus gigas*—Humboldt squid, jumbo squid, jumbo flying squid, *pota*, or *diablo rojo*
- *Nototodarus gouldi*—commonly called red arrow squid, Gould's squid, or Gould's flying squid

- *Ommastrephes bartramii*—commonly called neon flying squid, *akaika*, red squid, red ocean squid, red flying squid, flying squid, neon flying squid, or Bartram's squid
- *Sepioteuthis sepioidea*—commonly called Caribbean reef squid or reef squid
- *Sthenoteuthis oualaniensis*—commonly called purpleback flying squid, *tobiika*, or purple squid; and its orangeback cousin, *S. pteropus*
- *Todarodes pacificus*—commonly called Japanese flying squid, Japanese common squid, or Pacific flying squid.

War on Rats

**The South Pole: An Account of the Norwegian Antarctic
Expedition in the "Fram," 1910–1912**
Roald Amundsen, 1913

" We had a considerable collection of various families [on
board]: pigs, fowls, sheep, cats, and—rats. Yes, unfortunately,
we knew what it was to have rats on board, the most repulsive
of all creatures, and the worst vermin I know of. But we have
declared war against them, and off they shall go before the
Fram starts on her next voyage. We got them in Buenos Aires,
and the best thing will be to bury them in their native land. "

" Chapter XVI: The Voyage of the 'Fram' by First-Lieutenant
Thorvald Nilsen
Never since leaving Madeira (September 1910) had we
been troubled with animals or insects of any kind whatever; but when we were in Buenos Aires for the first time,
at least half a million flies came aboard to look at the vessel. I hoped they would go ashore when the *Fram* sailed;

but no, they followed us, until by degrees they passed peacefully away on fly-paper.

Well, flies are one thing, but we had something else that was worse—namely, rats—our horror and dread, and for the future our deadly enemies. The first signs of them I found in my bunk and on the table in the fore-saloon; they were certainly not particular. What I said on that occasion had better not be printed, though no expression could be strong enough to give vent to one's annoyance at such a discovery. We set traps, but what was the use of that, when the cargo consisted exclusively of provisions?

One morning, as Rönne was sitting at work making sails, he observed a 'shadow' flying past his feet, and, according to his account, into the fore-saloon. The cook came roaring: 'There's a rat in the fore-saloon!' Then there was a lively scene; the door was shut, and all hands started hunting. All the cabins were emptied and rummaged, the piano, too; everything was turned upside down, but the rat had vanished into thin air.

About a fortnight later I noticed a corpse-like smell in Hassel's cabin, which was empty. On closer sniffing and examination it turned out to be the dead rat, a big black one, unfortunately a male rat. The poor brute, that had starved to death, had tried to keep itself alive by devouring a couple of novels that lay in a locked drawer. How the rat got into that drawer beats me.

On cleaning out the provision hold nests were found with several rats in them: six were killed, but at least as many escaped, so now no doubt we have a whole colony. A reward was promised of ten cigars for each rat; traps were tried again, but all this did very little good. When we were in Buenos Aires for the second time we got a cat on board; it certainly kept the rats down, but it was shot on the Barrier. At Hobart we provided a few traps, which caught a good many; but we shall hardly get rid of them altogether until we have landed most of the provisions, and smoked them out. **”**

ACCORDING TO BART

Rats have an uncanny ability to lie low, which is why a three-pronged approach to pest control can be necessary. Seafurrers provide a complete catch-and-clean-up service, with an able-bodied seafurrer dealing with around three a day, but it will depend on the cat (some are more experienced than others) and the rats (wily old ones are a different ball game from the young and naive). There does seem to be a world ratter record. Naturalist Desmond Morris reckons in his book *Catwatching* that a tabby landlubber working at White City Stadium in London

from 1927 to 1933 holds it, raking in five or six a day for a grand total of 12,480 rats over the years of service. The only question about this tally is what did they count? Leftover tails?

Traps can be squeezed into very small spaces no ship's cat can get at. But they are a passive device—they need a passing rat to take the bait before they spring into action. And then someone has to retrieve the trap, dispose of the body, rebait, and replace it. There are also clever rats who seem to know how to get the bait and avoid the trap.

For serious infestations, the answer is smoking or fumigating, but back then these were jobs done in port. *Fram* wasn't back in port very often over the two years of the expedition. In that time she sailed two and a half times round the world, covering about 54,400 nautical miles and only stopping off in Madeira, Buenos Aires (three times), and Hobart, along with her main destination, the Bay of Whales, to drop off and collect the explorers.

Such adventures were all part of the "heroic age of Antarctic exploration"—heroic in the "doing it tough" sense, with few mechanical aids. Over some twenty years of trekking, trudging, climbing, mapping, and flag planting in Antarctica beginning in 1898, the power to pull sleds laden with kit and provisions was four legged—horses (Scott) or dogs (Amundsen, Shackleton, and Mawson), and/or two legged—men (Shackleton and Scott). Thirteen men died—washed overboard, fallen from a mast, fallen into a precipice, fallen through sea ice, starved, or frozen (the famous five of the Scott expedition). Two men from the Australasian Antarctic Expedition succumbed to nutritional diseases from the limited diet. Hypervitaminosis A (eating too much animal liver) took out Xavier Mertz, and Arnold Spencer-Smith died of scurvy (and cold).

For Amundsen, being first to the South Pole was the big one, the one that would give him fame and—more importantly—fortune to fund his plans for future Arctic exploration. He and his lot got to the pole thirty-three days before Scott's lot, planted the Norwegian flag on December 14, 1911, pitched a tent, left a note for Scott to deliver to the king of Norway (in case they were never seen again), and headed back to base, the waiting *Fram*, and home.

There's never been a tally of all the other animals (the nonhuman ones) who didn't make it home during the "heroic age." Numerous horses and dogs died or were slaughtered, and some were eaten. Mrs. Chippy, the ship's cat on Shackleton's icebound *Endurance*, was shot in 1915 because they couldn't take him to Elephant Island. (Mrs. Chippy's job was helping the ship's carpenter, Harry McNeish. "Chippy" is a British nickname for a carpenter. The "Mrs." was either a bloke joke or an inability to determine the sex of a cat.) It's an utter mystery why they shot *Fram*'s reliable ratter on the Barrier.

Incidentally . . .

The overkill question: Do cats kill because they are hungry, or is the urge to eat separate from the urge to kill? Curious about "reservoirs of neural energy," this is the sort of question scientists ask. Ethologist Paul Leyhausen is the man who did the fieldwork on this and published the classic book *Cat Behavior*. He gave mice to hungry and well-fed cats to see how long they would go on catching, killing, and eating them. Not too many surprises from what he found:

- Hungry cats killed and ate mice faster than well-fed cats.
- Hungry cats ate more mice than well-fed cats; some ate as many as twelve (reminiscent of people at a smorgasbord).

- Well-fed cats stopped eating mice at three—but kept on catching.
- After catching ten mice, there was a noted lack of enthusiasm all around, and all cats slowed down.
- After fifteen mice, all cats lost interest—and one mouse turned the tables and bit a cat on the paw.

Possibly all this experiment really showed was that:

- A hungry hunter will hunt until full to the brim and bored stiff.
- Some cats know when enough is enough.
- Farmers and millers knew they were onto a good thing when they employed cats as pest controllers.

To look at the "reservoirs of neural energy" question another way: Do *sapiens* hunters kill because they are hungry, or is the urge to eat separate from the urge to kill? With recreational hunting and fishing more popular than ever, it's more likely to be sport or trophy bagging than feeding the family, though fish, fowl, and other fauna (so long as it's not filled with shot) may be eaten after a spell in the family freezer.

Classic Catches

"Cat Catches Fish: Story from the Pacific"
Telegraph (Brisbane), December 28, 1926

'Believe it or not, this cat catches flying fish and provides portion of the sailors' diet,' said Mr. Gustave Green, chief officer of the Roosevelt Line steamer Cokesit to a representative of 'The Telegraph' on Tuesday. The chief officer's story was confirmed by Messds. Frank Brewer (second officer) and H. P. Simmons (third officer). They said that the cat sitting on the lower deck aft would reach up and seize a flying fish with its claws and mouth, then kill it by chewing its head, but save the body for the crew.

'The cat proved most difficult to train,' said the chief officer, 'but the trouble has proved worth while. It is a well known fact that flying fish often jump aboard vessels especially when passing through the Pacific Ocean. The fish is capable of flying at a height of 15 feet off the water. When the ship is fully loaded and is lying low in the water we frequently find a number of flying fish lying on the lower after deck. For some time, our cat Jenny got to the fish before we discovered them, and she commenced to make a meal of them. At first the members of the ship's company did not believe that Jenny caught the fish herself, but one evening an apprentice was patrolling the deck aft, when he saw Jenny reach up and seize a fish in the air. Jenny at first sat on the edge of the deck outside the rail when the fish were flying and tried to grab them. Now and again the fish would fly on to the deck, and Jenny evidently considered that she should not waste her energy catching them when they would come aboard of their own free will. She devoted her energies to catching the fish that came near the edge of the ship. After the cat had been punished a few times she realised that she was not allowed to eat the fish she caught and thus she became a benefactor to the officers and crew of the Cokesit.'

Jenny this afternoon blinked when the officers were recounting her performances.

"

ACCORDING TO BART

The occasional flying fish landing at your feet is as close to home delivery as you'll get at sea. Before tucking into fresh panfried fillets, people wax lyrical in journals and letters, as

it's spectacular to see them explode out of the water, take off, and soar, wings outstretched, above the waves. It even blew Sir Joseph Banks' mind:

> 1768 September 25. Wind continued to blow much as it had done so we were sure we were well in the trade; now for the

first time we saw plenty of flying fish, whose bea[u]ty especialy when seen from the cabbin windows is beyond imagination, their sides shining like burnishd silver; when seen from the Deck they do not appear to such advantage as their backs are then presented to the view, which are dark colourd.

But they aren't flying, says fish expert Frank Fish of West Chester University in Pennsylvania. They are gliding (there's a difference), using their pectoral and pelvic fins as wings:

To take to the air, a flying fish leaps from the water or rises to the surface continually beating its tail to generate propulsion as it starts to taxi. The taxiing run lets the fish accelerate at water surface and build momentum for take-off. Once the fish reaches its top speed of 20 to 40 miles an hour [32 to 64 kilometers per hour] it spreads its elongate fins and becomes airborne. . . .

The flight performance of these animals is impressive, with typical glides of 50 to 100 feet [15 to 30 meters] and flight times of 30 seconds. The fish can reach altitudes of 20 feet [6 meters]. Scientists hypothesize that the fish can increase distance and time aloft by using updrafts from the windward face of the waves. One report claimed that when flying into the wind a fish could travel over a quarter of a mile!

The trajectory of the glide by a flying fish is a flat arc, like that of some missiles. The French Exocet (the word means "flying fish" in French) [via Latin from Greek *ekōkoitos*, "fish that comes up on the beach"—literally "out of bed"] is a missile that skims just above the water surface before striking its target, usually a ship. Such a sea-skimming weapon caught the world's attention in 1982 when the British ship HMS Sheffield was sunk by an Exocet launched from an Argentinean naval aircraft [during the Falklands War, no lives lost].

At the end of the glide when speed and altitude are decreasing, flying fish can either fold up their wings and fall back into the sea or drop their tail into the water and reaccelerate for another flight. This capacity for successive flights greatly increases the possibilities for air time. The record reported is 12 consecutive flights covering 1200 feet [365 meters].

Firing Line to Fame

People's Dispensary for Sick Animals (PDSA)
Dickin Medal Award Citation

" Served on HMS Amethyst during the Yangtse Incident, disposing of many rats though wounded by shell blast. Throughout the incident his behaviour was of the highest order, although the blast was capable of making a hole over a foot in diameter in a steel plate. "

"Simon V.C."
News *(Adelaide), November 24, 1949*

" SIMON, the cat hero of HMS Amethyst and winner of the [PDSA] Dickin Medal (the animal's Victoria Cross) is resting quietly at Hackbridge Quarantine Kennels in Surrey until the frigate is refitted. The crew are being feted in England following their return from China where they were shelled by Communists. "

Signaller E. H. Wharton of Birmingham (left), telegraphist J. E. Welton of Chester (center), and Signaller J. E. Thomas of Breedon on the Hill, Leicestershire, (right) with Simon, DM

ACCORDING TO BART

Simon died in quarantine on November 28. Some say it was war wounds, others a broken heart. It was most likely feline enteritis. He was buried with full naval honors and farewelled by his shipmates at the PDSA's pet cemetery in Ilford, Essex.

HMS *Amethyst* had steamed up the Yangtze River from Shanghai to Nanjing to relieve the duty ship on April 19, 1949. It seems a bold decision during the Chinese Civil War with the People's Liberation Army on the north bank and the Kuomintang on the south. They came under a salvo of PLA fire at Jiangyin the very next day, with seventeen dead and ten wounded, including Simon and the captain. The captain later died of his wounds; medical attention and TLC got Simon back on his feet and on the job, and over the steamy 101 days the PLA held the ship hostage, he carried on with his duties. When negotiations failed, the *Amethyst* slipped her moorings on July 30 and made her escape in the dark.

Once free, Lieutenant Commander Kerans wasted no time nominating Simon for the PDSA's Dickin Medal for behavior of the highest order.

There were a large number of rats on board that began to breed rapidly in the damaged portions of the ship. They represented a real menace to the health of the ship's company. Simon nobly rose to the occasion and after two months the rats were much diminished. Throughout the Incident Simon's behaviour was of the highest order. One would not have expected him to have survived a shell making a hole over a foot in diameter in a steel plate, yet after a few days Simon was a friendly as ever. His presence on the ship, together with Peggy the dog, was a decided factor in maintaining the high level of morale of the ship's company. They gave the ship an air of domesticity and normality in a situation which in other aspects was very trying.

Back home, the crew was feted and Simon packed off to quarantine. This may be another first . . . on top of being the first cat to receive the PDSA Dickin Medal, and first Royal Navy animal to get one, he may well have been the first ship's cat to be "locked up" on landing. While "imported" cats and dogs were officially quarantined to keep rabies at bay from 1901 on, this seems to be the first record of a ship's cat heading to the isolation ward.

Britain had introduced strict dog controls in the late nineteenth century to deal with burgeoning numbers of stray dogs wandering the city streets and a seeming epidemic of "canine madness." By 1902 the tough-on-dogs policy paid off and the country was declared rabies-free. There was another outbreak after 1918 when British soldiers, who tend to collect dogs wherever they are stationed, smuggled in rabid dogs from the war zone (they didn't know they were rabid at the time, of course). The authorities got onto this promptly and Britain was rabies-free once again by 1922. Quarantine of all imported animals is how they kept it that way until the introduction of pet passports around 2001.

The idea of quarantine goes back to the Black Death or plague, which wiped out an estimated 30 percent of Europe's population, plus a goodly proportion of Asia's, in the middle of the fourteenth century. The word itself comes from the Italian *quaranta giorno*—"forty days." The Great Council of Ragusa (now Dubrovnik) set the quarantine ball rolling in 1377 with a law enforcing a thirty-day isolation period (*trentino*) for all newcomers (to see if symptoms of the Black Death developed) before they could enter the city. This was later extended to forty days, though no one is quite sure why.

Incidentally . . .

Hackbridge Kennels, mentioned in the Adelaide *News* story, has several claims to fame. It's where:

- Shackleton housed about one hundred sled dogs when preparing for his second Antarctic expedition
- They trained service dogs for the 1914–18 war effort
- They built five hundred isolation kennels for dogs the troops brought back from the front after the First World War.

MATES

"'If Maizie [the ship's cat] hadn't been with us, we might have gone nuts,' said Clancy. 'There's something about a dumb animal that takes your mind off trouble.' Maizie took her turn at mess, eating malted milk tablets and condensed foods with the crewmen. She even comforted the men suffering from exposure and seasickness, going from one to another almost like a mother, he said."

—*"Maizie, the Seagoing Cat,"* Lookout, *September 1943, quoting Eugene Clancy, rescued after fifty-six hours in a life raft with Maizie and five other crew members when their ship was torpedoed in the North Atlantic in March 1943*

WHISKIPEDIA

mate: a companion, comrade, friend, partner; a fellow worker

It's as a "friend" that *mate* arrived in the fourteenth century, borrowed from Middle German's *māt(e)* or *gemate* ("companion"). The word has Indo-European family ties to *mat* or *met* as in "measure" (a portion of food), making a mate someone to eat meat with, just as a companion is someone to break bread with (Latin *com* = "with"; *panis* = "bread"). *Mate* as an officer on a merchant ship and one of a wedded pair followed soon after.

Mate is a team player. It readily pairs with other words to describe the basis of a relationship, from classmates, crewmates, playmates, schoolmates, shipmates, teammates, and workmates to bunkmates, helpmates, housemates, and messmates—companions of the same mess table and comrades on board. "Whence the saw: 'Messmate before a shipmate, shipmate before a stranger, stranger before a dog,'" says William Henry Smyth in *The Sailor's Word-Book*.

Vital Victuals

A New Voyage Round the World
William Dampier, 1697

❝ [Setting out from Cape Corrientes for Guam, March 31, 1686]

We had not sixty days' provision, at a little more than half a pint of maize a day for each man [there were 100 men on the *Cygnet*] and no other provision except three meals of salted jew-fish; and we had a great many rats aboard, which we could not hinder from eating part of our maize. . . .

When we had eaten up our three meals of salted jew-fish in so many days' time we had nothing but our small allowance of maize. . . .

There was not any occasion to call men to victuals for the kettle was boiled but once a day, which being made ready at noon, all hands were aloft to see the quartermaster share it, wherein he had need to be exact, having so many eyes to observe him. We had two dogs

WHOM magazine

William Dampier: delicious buccaneer and lover of cats!

WHOM MAN of the Year 1686

and two cats aboard, they likewise lived on what was given them, and waited with as much eagerness to see it shared as we did. . . .

The 20th day of May . . . at four o'clock, to our great joy, we saw the island Guam. . . . It was well for Captain Swan that we got sight of it before our provision was spent, of which we had but enough for three days more; for, as I was afterwards informed, the men had contrived first to kill Captain Swan and eat him when the victuals was gone, and after him all of us who were accessory in promoting the undertaking this voyage. This made Captain Swan say to me after our arrival at Guam, 'Ah! Dampier, you would have made them but a poor meal;' for I was as lean as the captain was lusty and fleshy.

ACCORDING TO BART

Sharing meager rations with the ships' cats and dogs is true mateship, because a cup of maize boiled up with a bit of water each day isn't much to live on. It was probably just enough to keep the men going, although some were "weakened by it." It was probably around 500 calories (2,100 kJ), about a quarter of the average sailor's daily needs. As for supplementing their diet with a bit of fishing, no luck there. They saw no fish ("not so much as a flying-fish") or birds for five thousand miles.

Would they really have contrived to kill and eat Captain Swan and eat him when the victuals were gone? Possibly. Survivor cannibalism was not unknown, though unsurprisingly it was not widely

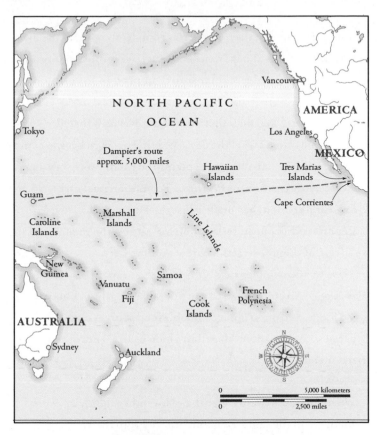

Dampier's route from Cape Corrientes to Guam

reported. William Boys' account some thirty years later on the loss of the *Luxborough* confesses that to stay alive the survivors were "impelled to adopt the horrible expedient of eating part of the bodies of our dead companions, and drinking their blood."

It surprises me that the *Cygnet*'s crew completely ignored the meat at their feet: the rats. They are just rodents like guinea pigs, squirrels, and beavers, and a regular source of protein for millions of animals of one kind or another. *Sapiens* spent thousands of years as hunter-gatherers, and their diet would have certainly included some sort of rodent if that's what the day's foraging brought back to camp for dinner. Polynesian navigators plying the Pacific were very happy to have *Rattus exulans* (*kiore*, or Pacific or Polynesian rats) on board, as skinned and roasted they made a tasty treat.

Reports of European sailors putting rats on the menu even in the direst of dietary straits are few and far between. This is no surprise to anthropologist Robin Fox, who says in *The Challenge of Anthropology*, "All cultures go to considerable lengths to obtain preferred foods, and often ignore valuable food sources close at hand."

Faced with starvation, Magellan's men didn't ignore them; they prized them:

> Wednesday, the twenty-eighth of November, 1520, we came forth out of the said strait, and entered into the Pacific sea, where we remained three months and twenty days without taking in provisions or other refreshments, and we only ate old biscuit reduced to powder, and full of grubs, and stinking from the dirt which the rats had made on it when eating the good biscuit, and we drank water that was yellow and stinking. We also ate the ox hides which were under the

main-yard, so that the yard should not break the rigging: they were very hard on account of the sun, rain, and wind, and we left them for four or five days in the sea, and then we put them a little on the embers, and so ate them; also the sawdust of wood, and rats which cost half-a-crown each, moreover enough of them were not to be got.

Louis-Antoine de Bougainville's crew also preferred to throw fresh rats into the cooking pot rather than risk rotten meat, well known for its dire and sometimes lethal consequences, on their voyage round the world (1766–69). So did the men on a French brig the Brits captured in 1800. "The Diligent [*La Diligence*] was full of rats. They were so numerous that the French seamen used to kill and cook them. . . . But I could not be prevailed upon to taste any," reported a squeamish Lieutenant William Dillon. Possibly this was a good call. Two years later, Lieutenant James Gardner related a cautionary tale of the perils of rat pie:

Our ship was full of rats, and one morning he [Marine Lieutenant Augustus Field] caught four which he had baked in a pie with some pork chops. When it came to table he began greedily to eat, saying, "What a treat! I shall dine like an alderman." One of our lieutenants (Geo. M. Bligh) got up from the table and threw his dinner up, which made Field say, "I shall not offend such delicate stomachs and

shall finish my repast in my cabin," which he did and we wished the devil would choke him. When he had finished, he said one of the rats was not exactly to his taste as the flesh was black; but whether from a bruise or from disease, he could not say, but should be more particular in future in the post mortem examination. I never was more sick in my life, and am so to this day when I think of it.

However, Gardner's tale has all the hallmarks of a tall story, plus a dash of hearsay and a scoop of anecdotal evidence—or all three. It could just as well have been a rotten pork chop. How can you tell when it's all cooked up in a pie?

Away Up Aloft!

"Matthew Flinders' Biographical Tribute to His Cat Trim"
Matthew Flinders, 1809

" The replacing a top-mast carried away, or taking a reef in the sails were what most attracted his [Trim's] attention at sea; and at all times when there was more bustle upon deck than usual, he never failed to be present and in the midst of it; for as I have before hinted, he was endowed with an unusual degree of confidence and courage, and having never received anything but good from men, he believed all to be his friends, and he was the friend of all. When the nature of the bustle upon the deck was not understood by him, he would mew and rub his back up against legs of one and the other, frequently at the risk of being trampled underfoot, until he obtained the attention of someone to satisfy him. He knew what good discipline required, and on taking in a reef, never presumed to go aloft until the order was issued; but go as soon as the officer had issued the word—'Away up aloft!'

Up he jumped along with the seamen, and so active and zealous was he, that none could reach the top before, or so soon as he did. His zeal, however, never carried him beyond a sense of dignity; he did not lay out on the yard like a common seaman, but always remained seated upon the cap, to inspect like an officer. This assumption of authority to which, it must be confessed, his rank, though great as a quadruped, did not entitle him amongst men, created no jealousy; for he always found some good friend ready to caress him after the business was done, and to take him down in his arms.

ACCORDING TO BART

The exhilaration of going aloft is hard to resist. Going up is a breeze; coming down less so, as Trim—Matthew Flinders' much-loved seafurrer who circumnavigated Australia—found. Chalk it up to the claw problem. Designed to shimmy up trees, fences, trellises, wooden power poles, carpeted scratching posts, and trouser legs, cats' claws curve toward the back rather like built-in crampons. Going up they do a great job; coming down, not so much—the claws are pointing the wrong way for getting a grip.

The savvy seafurrer has three options for the descent: thoughtful headfirst, discreet backing down, or hitching a ride—as Trim preferred. The angle of descent tends to be the decider for most seafurrers. Worst-case scenario? Jumping. It isn't always a nine-lives extreme challenge. Cats are designed to make a perfect landing on all four paws. Mostly.

How cats turn midair and land on their feet intrigued *sapiens* scientists in the nineteenth century. "How could a free-falling body change its orientation such that it is able to right itself as it falls to land on its feet, irrespective of its initial orientation, and without violating the law of conservation of angular momentum?" they asked. It seemed to defy Newtonian physics.

At Cambridge University in the 1850s, scientists apparently adopted the highly unethical approach of dropping cats out of windows to find out. James Clerk Maxwell wrote to his wife:

There is a tradition in Trinity [College] that when I was here I discovered a method of throwing a cat so as not to light on its feet, and that I used to throw cats out of windows. I had to explain that the proper object of research was to find how quick the cat would turn round, and that the proper method was to let the cat drop on a table or bed from about two inches, and that even then the cat lights on her feet.

Maxwell may have been a bit of a genius and gone on to become one of the nineteenth century's greatest theoretical physicists, but he never solved the "falling cat problem"—more a people problem of understanding than a cat problem, unless the cat happened to meet a physicist.

In 1894, French scientist and photographer Étienne-Jules Marey showed how falling cats turn midair and land on their feet in a series of images he captured at twelve frames per second on his chronophotographic gun and published in *Nature*. While he, too, was a cat thrower, at least it was not out of windows. He also made in 1894 what is probably the world's first cat movie: *Falling Cat*.

Within 0.125 to 0.5 of a second, a cat can safely turn over in its own standing height. In fact, "the speed and agility with which a cat turns over is truly wonderful," says Dr. Donald McDonald in *New Scientist*, where he describes a gold-medal performance that achieves a net rotation while keeping total angular momentum

MATES

constant and sticking the perfect landing. Of course, having a flexible backbone and no functional collarbone (clavicle) helps with such aerial acrobatics. As in all things, practice makes perfect, and experience is a great teacher.

Incidentally . . .

The righting reflex (also called air righting) begins to appear in kittens at three to four weeks of age, and they have perfected it by six to seven weeks.

Team Players

Ten "Old Salts": *Photograph taken on board USS Hartford at Hampton Roads, Virginia, winter 1876, by order of Chaplain David H. Tribou, US Navy*

(Front row, left to right) Seaman James H. Bell and Quartermaster Thomas Trueman; (second row, left to right) Boatswain's Mate Peter Eagen, Seaman Isaac Turner, and Schoolmaster James Connell; (rear row, left to right) Boatswain's Mate Edward Nash, Boatswain's Mate David Clark, Seaman William McNulty, Quarter Gunner William Harrington, and Gunner's Mate Albert Allen

ACCORDING TO BART

In the age of the selfie, taking photos is an everyday part of life. Back in 1876, photography was very much the new kid on the block, and it tended to involve rather cumbersome equipment. Early adopter Roger Fenton dragged his photography cart over Crimea in 1855, shooting battlefields, fortifications, and portraits of officers and men. Matthew Brady's bunch took it a step further, recording life on ships as well as in battlefields during the American Civil War (1861–65). They had more than seven thousand negatives when peace was declared.

Photography was the "documentary" game changer. David Tribou, one of the younger naval chaplains then on duty (appointed 1872), was interested in history and ended up Chaplain Corps historian with his own archive.

He was a man who liked to keep himself busy. As well as holding divine service on Sundays,

> he lectured to the men on the "history, government and resources of the islands" visited by the ship [USS *Powhatan*], and arranged for "friends from on shore" to give several concerts. The ship's library under his supervision, was "much enlarged during the year. . . ." Tribou tried to induce men "to abstain from the use of intoxicating liquors." He summarized his activities with this observation: "The work of a Chaplain which can be reported is but a small

part, and by far the least important part of his duty. While I have tried to attend to the more public duties, I have never lost sight of the fact that, in personal work among the men, lies the Chaplain's most promising opportunity, and while there is much to discourage one in such work yet it is by far the most satisfactory part of the work which I am sent to do."

Ten "Old Salts" is one of the earliest surviving "team player" photographs. We don't know why Tribou ordered the lineup, but it's easy to take an imaginative leap and guess he had copies printed for each of the men to send home to their families. It's unlikely he labeled the image *Old Salts*.

Tribou gets many tributes, but here's another for the record books: He knew it was important to have a pen and paper handy, as well as a camera, to name the team for posterity. Maritime archives are overflowing with unidentified or partially identified shipboard-life team shots. In 1893, on USS *New York*, Edward Hart not only shot the ships' tailors and their pets, as shown on page 94, but also the carpenters' gang, the champion boat crew, the crew of the forward 8-inch guns, and many more, but no one knows who they are.

Tailors of USS *New York* (from between 1893 and 1901)

All Aboard

Following the Equator: A Journey Around the World
Mark Twain, 1897

" Monday, December 23, 1895 . . . This *Oceana* is a stately big ship, luxuriously appointed. She has spacious promenade decks. Large rooms; a surpassingly comfortable ship. The officers' library is well selected; a ship's library is not usually that. . . . For meals, the bugle call, man-of-war fashion; a pleasant change from the terrible gong. . . . Three big cats—very friendly loafers; they wander all over the ship; the white one follows the chief steward around like a dog. There is also a basket of kittens. One of these cats goes ashore, in port, in England, Australia, and India, to see how his various families are getting along, and is seen no more till the ship is ready to sail. No one knows how he finds out the sailing date, but no doubt he comes down to the dock every day and takes a look, and when he sees baggage and passengers flocking in, recognizes that it is time to get aboard. This is what the sailors believe. "

 ACCORDING TO BART

Remarkable? Possibly. But it's unlikely this is really in the headline-grabbing "cat finds way home" category or that any ESP was involved. The answer is probably very straightforward. I'd imagine the *Oceana*'s cat disembarked to stretch his legs and hung around the dock to check out the local fare. He would be very familiar with the sounds, smells, and hustle and bustle of departure and know exactly when to stroll back on board, seemingly from nowhere.

There are numerous such stories, but generally there's going to be a commonsense explanation. Take Charles H. Ross' story in *The Book of Cats* (1868):

In 1819 a favourite Tabby belonging to a shipmaster was left on shore, by accident, while his vessel sailed from the harbour of Aberdour, Fife-shire [on the north shore of the Firth of Forth in Scotland], which is about half a mile from the village. The vessel was a month absent, and on her return, to the astonishment of the shipmaster, Puss came on board with a fine stout kitten in her mouth, apparently about three weeks old, and went directly down into the cabin. Two others of her young ones were afterwards caught, quite wild, in a neighbouring wood, where she must have remained with them until the return of the ship. The shipmaster did not allow her, again, to go on shore, otherwise it is probable she would have brought all her family on board. It was very remarkable, because vessels were daily going in and out of the harbour, none of which she ever thought of visiting till the one she had left returned.

Tabby may have been left behind, but it's more likely she headed down the gangplank as soon as the ship docked and over to the nearby woods to deliver her kittens in privacy. With a family to feed, she would then regularly be out and about hunting, and the port with its endless supply of rodents likely provided "easy pickings" on her daily rounds. Just because no one saw her swing by doesn't mean she didn't. It's unlikely she was on the lookout for her ship, but when it fortuitously docked, she just headed back on board for home comforts and family support. Who wouldn't?

Incidentally . . .

Sapiens are very dependent on their eyes to get their bearings. They also have maps and now GPS. Other animals don't need to be shown the way to go home like this because they use their senses. Which senses they use depends on the animal.

The sun and the stars shine for seabirds and migrating birds.

Magnetism matters for baby sea turtles, which typically migrate after hatching. A rather mean experiment that involved changing the orientation of magnetic generators around a swimming pool changed the direction in which the hatchlings swam, too (they were only babies).

The nose knows for felines and canines. But "the ability to find their way home depends in part on how far from home they get," reports animal behaviorist Dr. Bonnie Beaver of Texas A&M's College of Veterinary Medicine in a personal communication. She says:

In general dogs and cats have a relatively good sense of direction and use it to start their searches, but they depend on their senses for most navigation home. Because the home ranges of outdoor animals overlap, the animals are familiar with the smells of their neighbors. As the dog or cat randomly searches, it can begin orienting toward home once it picks up the familiar smell of the neighbor animal. As wanderings continue, it eventually picks up the smell of a second neighboring animal and can then orient more precisely.

It's worth remembering that some of the miraculous homecomings the press puts on the front page might simply be a case of mistaken identity or wishful thinking. "You hear these stories about a three-legged black cat that came home and jumped into its favorite chair," says Beaver. "But it's real hard to be sure because they've been gone a long time and they look scruffy. And heck, that chair would be a comfortable one for any cat."

Too right.

The Consolation of Pets

Through the First Antarctic Night, 1898–1899: A Narrative of the Voyage of the "Belgica" Among Newly Discovered Lands and over an Unknown Sea About the South Pole
Frederick Cook, 1900

" June 26.—It is Sunday; the weather is warm, wet, and too stormy to permit our usual Sabbath excursions. We are playing cards and grinding the music-boxes, and trying in various ways to throw off the increasing gloom of the night; but something has happened which has added another cloud to the hell of blackness which enshrouds us. One of the sailors brought with him from Europe a beautiful young kitten. This kitten has been named 'Nansen,' and it has steadily grown into our affections. 'Nansen' was at home alike in the forecastle and in the cabin, but with characteristic good sense he did not venture out on exploring trips. A temperature thirty degrees below zero was not to his liking; the quarters about the stove and the bed of a favourite sailor were his choice.

Since the commencement of the long darkness he has been ill at ease, but previously he was happy and contented, and glad to be petted and loved by everybody. The long night, however, brought out all the bad qualities of his ancestors. For nearly a month he has been in a kind of stupour, eating very little and sleeping much. If we tried to arouse him he displayed considerable anger. We have brought in a penguin occasionally to try to infuse new ambitions and a new friendship in the cat, but both the penguin and the cat were contented to take to opposite corners of the room. Altogether 'Nansen' seemed thoroughly disgusted with his surroundings and his associates, and lately he has sought exclusion in unfrequented corners. His temperament has changed from the good and lively creature to one of growling discontent. His mind has wandered and from his changed spiritual attitude we believe that his soul has wandered too. A day or two ago his life departed, we presume for more congenial regions. We are glad that his torture is ended, but we miss 'Nansen' very much. He has been the attribute to our good fortune to the present, the only speck of sentimental life within reach. We have showered upon him our affections, but the long darkness has made him turn against us. In the future we shall be without a mascot and what will be our fate?

MATES

Drawing of Nansen by cabin boy Johan Koren,
who brought Nansen on board *Belgica*, circa 1897

ACCORDING TO BART

It's about transitioning. Farm cats transitioned from pest controller to pet. The same happened with sea cats. Sailors were often so
devoted to their furry friends that they would hove to and row to
the rescue if a seafurrer fell overboard, as John Locke recorded in
1553 when the "shippes Cat lept into the Sea" (see page 137).

Their furry friends returned the favor. "Saved by a Cat from
Drowning: Feline Pet Scratches the Face of a Sleeping Man on a
Sinking Ship" was one headline in 1898:

PORT TOWNSEND. Nov. 27.—During a heavy storm that prevailed in the harbor last night the steamer Wildwood sank while lying at her dock. A large hole was made in her hull by a drifting log. A man who was asleep on board was saved from drowning by the ship's cat, which awakened him by scratching his face just as the steamer was going down.

Once upon a time, ships were so full of furry friends you would be forgiven for thinking them floating farmyards. There were cattle, pigs, goats, and poultry for fresh meat, eggs, and milk. And numerous pets. "The sailors, particularly those on board our ironclad men-of-war, are very partial to having pets at sea with them," the *People's Press* reassured its pet-loving readers in Winston-Salem, North Carolina, in 1892:

> This custom is not commonly forbidden by the commanding officers, for the life of a sailor is at best but a lonely and monotonous one, and he requires the companionship and recreation that are afforded by the presence of some animal. Some one of these pets is usually the favorite, and is acknowledged by all, from captain down to cabin boy, as a mascot.
>
> The mascot of the Baltimore is a goat. When she was put in commission he was duly entered on the vessel's papers as "William Goat." He is an old salt, having been

in Uncle Sam's navy since he was a kid. He will only consent to go ashore when the first cutter is lowered for "His Goatship," and he listens to the service every Sunday morning in as exemplary a manner as any of the other tars.

On board the Richmond at one time a hog was kept as a mascot. He had a bath every morning and always presented a neat appearance. His principal amusement consisted in pacing the deck with all the precision and dignity of an officer of the guard. He became almost too fat to move and was allowed to die a natural death.

Savvy editors quickly caught on that pet stories, whether tall tales or true, boosted sales. Tucked among ads for Rising Sun Stove Polish, Swamp-Root Kidney, Liver and Bladder Cure, and Tuft's Pills, in newspapers like the *People's Press* and the *Wray Rattler* (in Yuma County, Colorado), they filled column inches. YouTube, eat your heart out.

Vigilance

"Sailors Declare Cat Saved Ship from Ice:
Crew of Freighter Asserts Feline's Vigilance Was Responsible
for Their Safe Arrival in Port of Boston"
Los Angeles Herald, June 28, 1908

" BOSTON, June 27.—A common black cat, with a bob tail, dog-like ears and green eyes, saved the deeply laden British steamship Daltonhall from colliding with an iceberg off Cape Race. So at least say the crew of the ship, which is now berthed at Mystic wharf. The cat messes with the officers, which is another proof of the truth of the story. She answers to the name of 'Queen Lil' and is a native of Rotterdam.

Three weeks ago when the Daltonhall was at Rotterdam, Queen Lil came aboard and proceeded to make herself at home. Instead of making a beeline for the galley, as a cat might be expected to do, she seemed more interested in the engine room and the working of the telegraph, binnacle and steering gear. Indeed, the first thing Queen Lil did after boarding the ship was to make a tour of inspection. Evidently all was satisfactory, for she started with the steamer for Boston.

The freighter arrived in the ice region. The temperature had fallen and the water through which the ship was plowing was very cold. The cat was alert and so were the navigators. Her green eyes gleamed like coals and the doglike ears were cocked forward. She appeared to scent impending danger. The crew feared ice, and it was known the Daltonhall was hemmed by bergs and a collision might send her instantly to the bottom with all hands.

The seamen watched the cat, and the cat kept close to the navigators, all that weary night when double lookouts became almost blind for the time being by straining ahead for glimpses of bergs. After a sleepless vigil dawn revealed four bergs close to the ship. They were huge and colored a beautiful pale green with clouds of shadowy vapor floating above their glistening pinnacles. To have struck one of these formidable barriers would have been the death of the stout steel ship.

They feted the cat from Rotterdam and named her Queen Lil. Condensed milk was fed her from a spoon in honor of the deliverance from the icebergs. "

ACCORDING TO BART

A hunter's vigilance and ability to monitor surroundings comes in handy standing watch. While there's a popular saying that cats can see in the dark, it's not entirely true—not total dark. Cats can see in near darkness where *sapiens*' eyes are useless, because feline eyes are designed to be highly efficient at capturing whatever light is around. It's about size. A cat's eyes are very big compared with the size of its head; in dim light, the iris, or colored portion, can open very wide to let in as much light as possible.

Cats' eyes also have a special reflective layer at the back called the tapetum. This has a very specific job: reflecting any incoming light that the receptor cells miss right back to the retinal cells, which enhances sensitivity by some 40 percent. This also explains why a cat's eyes glow in the dark when they catch the light.

Then there are the rods and cones. They turn incoming light into electrical signals. Rods are for black-and-white vision in dim light, and cones are for color vision in bright light. Cats have more rods, humans more cones. But there's more to the story. In humans, each rod connects to a single nerve; in cats, the rods merge and are connected in bundles. What this adds up to is cats have ten times fewer nerves than humans traveling between their eyes and their brains, which consolidates the energy in low light and allows cats to see when there's very little light around.

When one ship's cat led its crew to safety after their small boat capsized in Grangemouth (Firth of Forth, Scotland) in 1920, the journalist on the spot put it down to feline intuition and wanting to get home and dry:

Nine men of the crew of the American cargo steamer Lake Eliko were saved from drowning recently by the instinct of the ship's cat to swim toward the steamer in a storm and darkness when their small boat foundered at midnight between the ship and the shore.

John Shortne, a sailor, and Gilmer Stroud, a mess room boy, were drowned.

The 11 members of the crew had been ashore on leave. They had with them the ship's cat. A storm began while they were ashore and when they were some distance out on their return journey to the steamer their boat capsized. In the darkness no one could make out the lights of the ship.

Tabby, however, with her instinctive desire to get out of the water as quickly as possible, swam directly toward the steamer. The men swam after her and nine of them reached the ship. The other two went down.

It's more likely that Tabby could (a) make out the lights of the steamer in the darkness when the crew couldn't and (b) sense things the crew was oblivious to. On top of this, her very sensitive hearing would help her pinpoint the direction sound was coming from—the steamer would certainly have had engines running.

Sleeping Quarters

Diary of the Terra Nova Expedition
to the Antarctic 1910–1912
Edward Wilson

" [Monday, October 17, 1910] The Admiral and his officers came on board early and we were all introduced and trotted him round. He was a most intelligent questioner and seemed to go to the heart of every detail at once and was very pleasant. Our cat was inspected. We have a small muscular black cat . . . who came on board as an almost invisible kitten in London or Cardiff. He has grown stiff and small and very strong and has a hammock of his own with the 'hands' under the fo'c's'le. The hammock is about 2 ft long with proper lashings and everything made of canvas. A real man o' war hammock with small blankets and a small pillow, and the cat was asleep in his hammock with his black head on the pillow and the blankets over him. The Admiral was much amused and while he was inspecting the sleeping cat, [he] opened his eyes, looked at the Admiral, yawned in his face and stretched out one black paw and then went back to sleep again. It was a very funny show and amused the Admiral and his officers as much as anything. [He] has learned to jump into his hammock which is slung under the roof along with the others and creeps in under the blanket with his head on the tiny pillow. "

ACCORDING TO BART

The full story behind why the "small muscular black cat" was so sleepy is that he had turned in early, "not feeling very well, owing to the number of moths he had eaten, the ship being full of them." When he was suddenly awakened for an entirely unexpected inspection by the admiral commanding the Australian Station, he had no idea of the importance of the occasion; how could he? No wonder he stretched, yawned, turned over, and went back to sleep.

Felines need an average of fifteen or sixteen hours of sleep a day. No surprises there, as it's a typical sleeping pattern for hunters who need to keep the sleep tank topped up, spreading it over the day in

- Catch-up catnaps
- Longer light sleeps (which drift into)
- Short bouts of deep sleep.

SIX. BELL SLEEPER
WYOMING'S MASCOT

Six Bell Sleeper, mascot of USS *Wyoming*, on a postcard from the ship while at sea, dated July 8, 1913

As for hammocks, they were another Columbus "discovery." Along with peppers and pineapple, he brought them back from the Old World to the New. Wikipedia's "Hammock" entry tells us he came across them on his first voyage when "a great many Indians in canoes came to the ship to-day for the purpose of bartering their cotton, and *hamacas*, or nets, in which they sleep."

It didn't take long for the naval powers-that-be to figure out these woven sleeping nets were an ideal way to fit many men into a small space for a night's sleep. Better still, they could be taken down and stowed during the day, clearing the decks for battle, blockade, or other seafaring or warfaring business. And they did double duty as shrouds: A sailor who died at sea would be sewn up in his hammock and tossed overboard with due rites.

It's possible Spain shared the benefits of hanging beds during a brief period of cordial relations between warring nations around 1554, when Philip I wedded and bedded Mary I of England. However, the Royal Navy didn't make them regulation bedding until 1597.

Although sleeping arrangements were cramped and a hammock no luxury bed, young midshipman Basil Hall fondly recalled the "cozy" nest on HMS *Leander* that gave him the soundest sleep:

> Most people, I presume, know what sort of a thing a hammock is. It consists of a piece of canvass, five feet long by two wide, suspended to the deck overhead by means of two sets of small lines, called clews, made fast to grummets, or rings of rope, which, again, are attached by a lanyard to the battens stretching along the beams. In this sacking are placed a small mattress, a pillow, and a couple of blankets, to which a pair of sheets may or may not be added. The degree of nocturnal room and comfort enjoyed by these young gentlemen may be understood, when it is mentioned that the whole of the apparatus just described occupies less than a foot and a half in width, and that the hammocks touch one another. Nevertheless, I can honestly say, that the soundest sleep, by far, that I have ever known, has been

found in these apparently uncomfortable places of repose; and though the recollection of many a slumber broken up, and the bitter pang experienced on making the first move to exchange so cozy a nest, for the snarling of a piercing north-west gale on the coast of America, will never leave my memory, yet I look back to those days and nights with a sort of evergreen freshness of interest, which only increases with years.

Incidentally . . .

The English *hammock* comes via the Spanish *hamaca* from the Taíno *hamaka* (the language of the first indigenous peoples Columbus encountered in the Caribbean). Woven sleeping nets or hanging beds were what the original inhabitants of Central and South America slept in and were also known as "brasill beds" or "Indian beds." Gonzalo Fernández de Oviedo y Valdés in his *Historia general y natural de las Indias* (Seville, 1535) says:

> The Indians sleep in a bed they call an "hamaca" which looks like a piece of cloth with both an open and tight weave, like a net . . . made of cotton . . . about 2.5 or 3 yards long, with many henequen twine strings at either end which can be hung at any height. They are good beds, and clean . . . and since the weather is warm they

require no covers at all . . . and they are portable so a child can carry it over the arm.

Hamacas were also fishing nets. The redoubtable Wikipedia suggests that whether for fishing or sleeping, these early hammocks from Mexico and the Caribbean were "woven out of bark from a hamack tree." That seems logical, possibly too logical. On investigation, this "hamack tree" is more likely native to a widespread digital species thriving in numerous internet sites rather than a botanical species indigenous to the Americas.

More likely sources for the fibers for weaving hammocks were *Agave fourcroydes* (henequen) and *Furcraea andina* (*fique* or *cabuya*). In *A Voyage to the Islands Madera, Barbados, Nieves, S. Christophers and Jamaica*, Sir Hans Sloane said:

> The *Magurie*-Tree or *Cabuya*, yields Wine, Vinegar, Honey, Beds, Threads, Needles, (out of the prickles of the Leaves) Tables, and Hafts of Knives, besides many medicinal uses. . . . *Oviedo* in his *Coronica de las Indias* . . . tells us that they make of this and *Henequen*, or Silk-Grass, good Ropes. The Leaves are laid in Rivers, and covered with Stones, as Flax in *Spain*, for some days, then they dry them in the Sun, after clear them of filth, with which they make many things, including *Hamacas*, some of this is white, others reddish.

Not a hamack tree in sight.

For good measure, English is indebted to Taíno for numerous words, usually via the Spanish given here:

- barbecue: *barbacoa*
- maize: *maíz*
- hurricane: *huracán*
- savanna: *zavana*
- tobacco: *tabaco*.

Mateship

*North Sea. Some Crew Members of Battlecruiser
HMAS Australia (I) Displaying Winter Protective Clothing Worn
During North Sea Operations from 1915 to 1918*

The photographer probably couldn't believe his luck when one of the crew arrived with a seafurrer stuffed in his vest. Wartime photographers early on sussed out the symbolic value of a pet in the picture. The ship's cat was a particularly popular "prop" for official (and unofficial) photographers and starred in hug shots, mug shots, hat shots, gun shots, shoulder shots, and hammock shots. Amid bad news of bombs and body counts, seeing photos of seafurrers taking it all in stride reassured folks back home that "our hardened men at sea" were doing just fine with their seafurring shipmates.

The title of the photo is all the caption for this classic reveals. No names, no date, though it was likely the winter of 1916–17, as that's when HMAS *Australia* was on regular patrols with the British Grand Fleet in the North Sea. As for the lineup, maybe "Seaman Clark," who loaned it to the Australian War Memorial to copy for their collection, is one of the men on deck? Or maybe not. We'll never know.

While many shots were stage-managed, there's no stage-managing tucking a cat in a vest. Seafurrers aren't normally very enthusiastic about restraint, since they need to be free to come and go to check their territory.

That said, seafurrers aren't averse to body contact, and for a bit of extra warmth will happily spread over the end of the bed. That's exactly what Winston Churchill's black cat Nelson did twenty-five years later in another world war. He regularly curled up on the great man's feet at the end of his bed as he worked. Nelson "does more for the war effort than you do," joked Churchill with colleague Rab Butler, president of the Board of Education. "He acts as a hot water bottle and saves fuel and power." Nelson in fact played an even more vital wartime role—he ensured Britain's PM during the Second World War did not get cold feet.

Incidentally . . .

Pets were very much a feature of life at sea in both world wars. Gilbert Adshead, engine room artificer in HMS *Lord Nelson* in the Eastern Mediterranean during the Gallipoli campaign (February 1915 to January 1916), recalled they had several pets on board, including:

> a pigeon; a couple of canaries; a black cat; a white cat; a bulldog, who was mascot of the football team; a Manchester terrier, a lady, who eventually begat herself a family when we were refitting and brought them all on board as well; and we had early, at the beginning of the war, a goat. Oh, and we had a monkey. He was a nice fellow old Jacko. . . .

Jobs for the Girls

The catering crew of SS Newcastle, a paddle steamer that did the overnight run between Sydney and Newcastle (New South Wales, Australia) for forty years. Sydney, circa 1910–20

Jobs for the girls on the ocean waves were few and far between in the age of sail. It was a strictly male preserve, *sapiens*-wise. That's not to say there were never women on board. There were on occasion wives and daughters as well as women who disguised themselves as men to get a job at sea. On the seafurring side, there were countless top-notch, able-bodied female sea cats often reckoned to be far better mousers.

Steam changed all that. Regular mail and passenger steamer services created more and different jobs, including entire catering departments. And it created jobs only women could do in those days—catering to "the ladies."

The *Times* (London) described the Margate-to-London paddle steamer *Thames* on July 8, 1815:

> Her cabins are spacious, and are fitted up with all that elegance could suggest, or personal comfort require; presenting as choice library, backgammon boards, draught tables, and other means of amusement. For the express purpose of combining delicacy with comfort a female servant attends upon the ladies.

"Ladies will have a female steward to wait on them," announced the *Talbot*, a cross-Channel steamer that ran from London to Calais in the summer of 1822.

Women also did the washing and ironing and mending (no surprises here). "When the ship is lying at any foreign port, the stewardesses are to be constantly employed, and every opportunity must be taken by them to keep the ship's linen in order," decreed the Cunard Line's rule book.

But the men and women had to be kept apart. "I am convinced that it is a very desirable thing to have a woman of character and experience in the position of a matron on board every emigrant ship carrying single women," proclaimed Thomas Gray, assistant secretary of the Marine Department in his report to the president of the UK Board of Trade in 1881:

> Such a woman in her capacity of matron ought to act as a general supervisor of the comfort and conduct of the single women in the steerage. She should play the part of an ever present domestic inspector, and her special office should be to encourage decency and order and suppress any indecorum amongst the single females.

Such a matron had her work cut out for her. Sarah Elizabeth Stephens, emigrating to New Zealand from Wales on the *Cardigan Castle*, jotted down in her diary a typical hazard the chastity enforcer faced.

[October 16, 1876] . . . Some of the girls have been breaking the rules by writing notes to the sailors. The matron came up unexpectedly and tried to take the letter from them. There was a scuffle in which the Matron's hat (a new one) fell overboard and some knitting she had in her hand. She is very angry. I do not know what will be done with the girls.

Able-Bodied Seafaring Cat Wanted

"A Feline A.B. Cat Sails Round the World: Captain's Interesting Story"
Daily News (Perth, Western Australia), February 8, 1923

"Purring softly in a cosy arm-chair in the skipper's cabin was a huge black tomcat. Edwin Dyason, captain of the freighter Woodfield, which is lying at the North Wharf, patted the animal's head, and turning to 'The Daily News' reporter standing alongside, expatiated earnestly on the virtues of seafaring cats. Captain Dyason is a firm believer in the feline species, or at least those cats that go down to the sea in ships. He is of the opinion that the complement of his ship is not in order if a cat is not on the pay-roll. Having for the last 27 years been a ship's master, his ideas on the subject should carry weight, and he brought all his maritime experience to bear when he discussed seafaring cats with our representative yesterday.

'We were at Fremantle about 12 months ago,' said he, 'and the day we left a lean grey she-cat leaped from the wharf on to the deck. We called her Cleopatra, and like Cleopatra of ancient history, she was mistress of all she surveyed. She strode the deck in the roughest weather, had free access to the scullery, slept in the cosiest spots, and woe betide the individual who attempted to disturb her. From Fremantle we went to the United Kingdom, then to Bombay, and back to England again, and Cleopatra was still queen of the ship. Our next port was New York, but, alas, the gleaming bright lights of Broadway gave Cleo a far away glimpse of a gay life, and she left us flat.

'We picked up general cargo at New York for Manila and China, and from other instructions I knew that our cruise would take us round the world, starting at, and returning to, Fremantle. But we had no cat. I was at my wits' end. During the last day in port I ordered two sailors to scour the wharfside for an able bodied seafaring cat, but landlubbers were all that they could locate, and it really looked as if we would have to sail without a dumb shipmate. A friend offered me a fine Angora kitten, but I declined the gift, only seagoing cats were of any use. We cleared New York the following morning, but as we took up the gangway a black Tom sauntered nonchalantly up and on to the deck. Since then we have been in Manila, Japan, China, Nauru, and Newcastle, and the cat has stuck to us all the way.'

The captain again stroked the sleek fur of the reclining cat, and as the animal purred appreciatively, he tackled the question of seafaring cats from the angle of personal experience.

'Sea cats are a race in themselves. A landlubber cat would not know how to take care of itself in a rough sea, but a sailor cat knows just what pile of ropes to hide under. It stays there and waits for fair weather before it reappears to demand rations. The seafaring cat is no joke. What is more, plenty of them have never been on shore, at all. They are born at sea, live on ships, and when they die they go down to Davy Jones' locker. Almost every time we start on a voyage we find one or more strange cats on board. They often change ships, but seldom give up the sea for the land. Indeed I have never heard of a sailor cat doing so. Sometimes when several cats are aboard they assign parts of the ship to themselves, and will not allow others within their particular precincts. One old boy we had kept every cat aft but himself, and proud he was of his power to do so.

'I know where the term "jealous cat" originated. I once had a cat—my favorite of all—named Margaret. She became so attached to me that she would not allow the other cats aboard to go into my cabin. She was even jealous of her kittens. No, Sir, ship's cats and the ordinary domestic variety appear to be of two distinct species. I was certain that a cat would replace the capricious Cleopatra before we left the New York dock, but must confess to feeling a little uneasiness towards the end. But sure enough "Tommy" here bobbed up of his own free will, having decided in his clever feline mind that he would like to join for the voyage.'

ACCORDING TO BART

While the gleaming, bright lights of Broadway may well have appealed to Dyason and his crew, it's doubtful they ever beckoned Cleopatra. It's more likely she simply yearned for fresh horizons and voyages on other ships involving fewer rats and more flying fish. She wasn't capricious. She was just exercising free will and a natural inclination to explore. When you think of the size of a feline's natural home range, it's not too surprising that seafurrers sometimes balk at the restrictions of shipboard life with all its barriers, bulwarks, doors, and hatches.

Some readers may be taken aback at Dyason's "dumb" reference. In this day and age, it seems an insensitive way to describe a shipmate. But Dyason doesn't mean to offend—he's simply using the word in the "lack of spoken language" sense that was common at the time. It does, however, highlight his anthropocentric orientation.

Cats most certainly talk. We talk to each other and to *sapiens* with a very specific array of sounds, scents, body language, facial expressions, and marks to express our feelings and needs. This "language" may not facilitate a deep and meaningful philosophical conversation, but then many people aren't up to that, either, despite having words and sentences to communicate with.

Konrad Lorenz (another ethologist) perceptively pointed out that "there are few animals in whose faces an observer can so clearly read a prevailing mood and predict what actions—friendly or hostile—are likely to follow" as in a cat's. It's very true—felines find it hard to dissemble, to hide their feelings. Their human companions, of course, have to be open to learning how to read them.

"Are we smart enough to know how smart animals are?" is the real question to ask, according to one of *Time* magazine's 100 Most Influential People in 2007, ethologist Frans de Waal, in the title of his 2016 bestselling book.

MISADVENTURES

"An extraordinary thing happened during the night. The tabby cat—Mrs. Chippy—jumped overboard through one of the cabin portholes and the officer on watch, Lt. Hudson, heard her screams and turned the ship smartly round and picked her up [with biologist Robert Clarke's net]. She must have been in the water 10 minutes or more."

—*Thomas Orde Lee's diary, September 13, 1914*

misadventure: an unfortunate incident; a mishap

Cats are hunters, and hunters venture forth and have adventures, or "that which happens by chance, fortune, luck." Of course there's a fair bit of planning and good management with successful hunting.

William the Conqueror was a hunter of sorts. He was country hunting when he crossed the channel with his Norman knights to take on King Harold at the Battle of Hastings in 1066. The arrow that took out Harold square in the head could be called "death by misadventure." Or what happens when things turn out badly in battle.

William not only brought Norman law and order to England, he brought French words that found their way into English. *Adventure* (*aventure*) was one; *misadventure* (*mesaventure*) another. But the English, who like to put their own stamp on things, went back to the Latin and added the *d* the French had dropped.

"All under the Sunne are subject to worldly miseries and misadventures," said Sir Walter Raleigh. He should have added that it's much more likely at sea where worse things regularly happen. As Samuel Johnson pointed out: "No man will be a sailor who has contrivance enough to get himself into jail; for being in a ship is being in a jail, with the chance of being drowned."

There was certainly much misadventure and death by misadventure. On the bright side, there was also *rescue*, from an Old French word, *rescourre*, meaning to free, deliver, or save (*re* + *escourre*; "to pull away, shake, drive out, remove").

Wreck Rights

Statute of Westminster, 1275

> Concerning wreck of the sea, it is agreed, that where a man, a dog, or a cat escape quick [alive] out of a ship, that such ship nor barge, nor anything within them, shall be ajudged wreck; but the goods shall be saved and kept by view of the sheriff, coroner, or king's bailiff, and delivered into the hands of such as are of the town where the goods were found; so that if any sue for these goods, and after prove that they were his, or perished in his keeping, within a year and a day, they shall be restored to him without delay; and if not they shall remain to the king.

ACCORDING TO BART

A cat or dog equal to "a man"! If not the first, it must be one of the earliest pieces of animal rights legislation. Though of course this isn't about animal rights; it's about "finders, keepers" and who gets what after a shipwreck, if there's anything left to get.

So, what was left to get? On just one day, December 5, 1388, fishermen from the tiny village of Sizewell in Suffolk, England, reported their findings and their values in the local "wreck book."

An oar	14 pence
A barrel	3 pence
Trestles and poor-quality wood	6 pence
60 pieces firewood	4 pence

While spats about divvying up the spoils of "wreck" have filled law books over the years, there's been remarkably little comment on why surviving cats and dogs were included in this legislation. Cats were part of the ship's crew and ran the pest-control department, so no surprises there, though how they would claim a share of "wreck" as survivors is a bit of a mystery. Dogs were often passengers or pets on merchant ships, probably the master's. While they didn't help run the ship, they were very useful in keeping things running smoothly by providing a bit of companionship and keeping spirits up on long absences from home. Even short distances in the days of sail could mean long absences due to inclement weather and winds. And all too often the men never did get home but were shipwrecked.

In the British navy, dogs were a fixture for several hundred years until the 1974 Rabies (Importation of Dogs, Cats and Other

Mammals) Order put an end to a way of life. Matthew Flinders in his tribute to his cat Trim reported in 1809 that they had several dogs on board, but

Trim was undisputed master of them all. When they were at play upon the deck, he would go in amongst them with his stately air; and giving a blow at the eyes of one, and a scratch on the nose to another, oblige them to stand out of his way. He was capable of being animated against a dog, as dogs usually may be against a cat; and I have more than once sent him from the quarter deck to drive a dog off the forecastle. He would run half the way briskly, crouching like a lion which has prey in view; but then assuming a majestic deportment, and without being deterred by the menacing attitude of his opponent, he would march straight up to him, and give him a blow on the nose, accompanied with a threatening mew! If the dog did not immediately retreat, he flew at him with his warcry of Yow! If resistance was still made, he leaped up on the rail over his head and so bespattered him about the eyes that he was glad to run off howling. Trim pursued him till he took refuge below; and then returned smiling to his master to receive his caresses.

Why so many dogs? "A dog is the most obvious and natural pet for a gentleman," according to naval officer, traveler, and author Basil Hall. Officers would embark with a dog or two in tow or acquire one or more at sea, sometimes as the spoils of war, sometimes as a souvenir of a tour of duty. When HMS *Salisbury* was stationed at St. John's in Newfoundland in 1785, Newfoundlands were the "dog du jour." The admiral gave permission for any person that pleased to take home a dog but was possibly surprised to see seventy-five march up the gangplank. Midshipman James Gardner was on the spot.

I messed in the main hatchway berth on the lower deck, with four midshipmen and a scribe. We had eight of those dogs billeted on us. One of them had the name of Thunder. At dinner I once gave him a piece of beef with plenty of mustard rolled up in it. The moment he tasted it, he flew at me and I was obliged to run for it. He never forgot it, and whenever I offered him victuals he would snap at me directly. Another of those dogs used to sleep at the foot of Charley Bisset's cot, and when the quartermaster would call the watch this dog would fly at him if he came near Bisset, who would often plead ignorance of being called, and by that means escape going on deck for the first hour of the watch.

Incidentally . . .

Shipwreck jargon:

- Wreck: goods that end up on the shore
- Flotsam: property still awash at sea
- Jetsam: sunken goods thrown overboard to save the ship
- Ligan: sunken goods tied to a buoy or cork to facilitate recovery.

Swings and Roundabouts

"The Voyage of M. John Locke to Jerusalem"
**The Principal Navigations, Voyages, Traffiques and
Discoveries of the English Nation**
Richard Hakluyt, 1598–1600

" I John Locke, accompanied with Maister Anthony Rast-
wold, and divers other, Hollanders, Zelanders, Almaines
and French pilgrimes entered the good shippe called Fila
Cavena of Venice, the 16 of July 1553. and the 17 in the
morning we weighed our anker and sayled towardes the
coast of Istria, to the port of Rovigno, and the said day
there came aboard of our ship the Percevena of the shippe
named Tamisari, for to receive the rest of all the pilgrimes money, which was in all after the rate of 55.
Crownes for every man for that voyage, after the rate of
five shillings starling [sterling] to the crowne: This done,
he returned to Venice. . . .

[August] The 18. Day. . . . It chanced by fortune that
the shippes Cat lept into the Sea, which being downe, kept

her selfe very valiauntly above water, notwithstanding the great waves, still swimming, the which the master knowing, he caused the Skiffe with halfe a dosen men to goe towards her and fetch her againe, when she was almost halfe a mile from the shippe, and all this while the ship lay on staies. I hardly beleeve they would have made such haste and meanes if one of the company had bene in the like perill. They made the more haste because it was the patrons cat. This I have written onely to note the estimation that cats are in, among the Italians, for generally they esteeme their cattes, as in England we esteeme a good Spaniell. The same night about tenne of the clocke the winde calmed, and because none of the shippe knewe where we were, we let fall an anker about 6 mile from the place we were at before, and there wee had muddie ground at twelve fathome.

ACCORDING TO BART

Don't bank on staying esteemed. Today's A-lister, tomorrow's has-been—it's all part and parcel of fortune's swings and roundabouts. Take spaniels. They may have been highly esteemed lap dogs in John Locke's England, but where are they now? Not ruling the internet. That's for cats. For now. Tomorrow? Who knows?

"Cat-friendly" is not how you would describe Locke's Europe. He was plum in the middle of grim times when, as Donald Engels puts it in *Classical Cats*, "millions of cats and hundreds of thousands of their female owners were brutally tortured and slain throughout western Europe during the Great Cat Massacre and the associated witchcraft hysteria." No wonder Locke was surprised they stopped the boat.

Venice was different. Always. A busy, cosmopolitan port built on trade with East and West had little time for witch-hunting, which never really caught on in the sophisticated intellectual and cultural world that grew from Renaissance Italy. Seafaring Venetians continued to buck the trend and esteem their cats for their pest-control prowess, signing on seafurrers to ensure their cargoes were delivered fit for sale and everyone got paid.

Doge of Venice Generalissimo Francesco Morosini was inordinately fond of his cat, a valiant seafurrer who took part in his campaigns against the Ottoman Empire, standing shoulder to shoulder on the poop deck to reconquer Athens and the Peloponnese. What Morosini is mostly remembered for today, however, is destroying the Parthenon (1687). The Turks were using it as a gunpowder store, and he shelled it. You could say his reputation took a hit with this.

Esteem has stuck to scholar and priest Richard Hakluyt, who brings us Locke's story. While no seafarer and never voyaging farther than Paris, his publications tell tales of adventure and courage on the high seas and have inspired generations of explorers, sailors, and armchair travelers. His travel-writing career began with a teenage light bulb moment. An older cousin sparked his lifelong passion for geography, telling him about recent discoveries and new opportunities for trade and showing him "certeine bookes of Cosmographie, with an universall Mappe."

That did it. He resolved from then on to "prosecute that knowledge and kinde of literature" at university. He entered Christ Church, Oxford, in 1570, carried out his intended course of reading and, by degrees, covered all the printed or written voyages and discoveries he could find, as well as taking his BA in 1574 and MA in 1577. At some stage he gave public lectures in geography that "shewed both the olde imperfectly composed, and the new lately reformed Mappes, Globes, Spheares, and other instruments of this Art." He was an early adopter.

The Principal Navigations, Voyages, Traffiques and Discoveries of the English Nation, first printed in one volume in 1589 and then as a greatly expanded three-volume edition in 1598–1600, was a compendium of voyages from ancient times. *Prodigious* is the only word to describe his achievement in compiling and editing hundreds of documents, from accounts of diplomatic and trade missions to translations of foreign works, letters patent, and travelers' tales such as John Locke's, within its pages.

Incidentally . . .

On the occasion of his traveler's tale, John Locke (also spelled Lok) was on a pilgrimage to the Holy Land, something likely to hold him in high esteem in Mary I's England, where she was busily stoking the pyres to turn back the Protestant clock.

But Locke is not an ideal candidate to be the pinup boy for a pilgrim's progress. The following year, wearing a very different hat, he set sail from London for Guinea as captain of a trading voyage that brought home with them, according to Hakluyt's account, "certaine blacke slaves, whereof some were tall and strong men, and could wel agree with our meates and drinkes."

The plan was to teach the slaves English so they could act as interpreters on future trading voyages to Guinea. We don't know if those slaves ever saw their homes again, but after that numerous charters were granted to British merchants to establish settlements on the West Coast of Africa to supply ivory, gold, pepper, dyewood, and indigo. These weren't the only commodities they traded. Slaves proved the most profitable venture for Elizabethan sea dogs like John Hawkins, Francis Drake, and the countless slave traders who followed.

Thus began Britain's role in the infamous Atlantic triangular slave trade, a three-legged journey for British slave traders. They took:

- manufactured trade goods—cloth, guns, ammunition, beads, alcohol—to West Africa to barter for slaves
- slaves (men, women, and children captured by slave traders or bought from African chiefs) across the Atlantic (in the stage of trade known as the Middle Passage) to sell in the West Indies and North American colonies
- sugar, rum, molasses, tobacco, and hemp back to Britain.

Designated Diver

The Journal of a Voyage to Lisbon
Henry Fielding, Esq, 1755

" *Thursday, July 11. . . .* A most tragical incident fell out this day at sea. While the ship was under sail, but making, as will appear, no great way, a kitten, one of four of the feline inhabitants of the cabin, fell from the window into the water: an alarm was immediately given to the captain, who was then upon deck, and received it with the utmost concern and many bitter oaths. He immediately gave orders to the steersman in favour of the poor thing, as he called it; the sails were instantly slackened, and all hands, as the phrase is, employed to recover the poor animal. I was, I own, extremely surprised at all this; less, indeed, at the captain's extreme tenderness, than at his conceiving any possibility of success; for if puss had had nine thousand, instead of nine lives, I concluded they had been all lost. The boatswain, however, had more sanguine hopes; for, having stript himself of his jacket, breeches, and shirt, he leapt boldly into the water, and, to my great astonishment, in a few minutes, returned to the ship, bearing the motionless animal in his mouth. Nor was this, I observed, a matter of such great difficulty as it appeared to my ignorance, and possibly may seem to that of my fresh-water reader: the kitten was now exposed to air and sun on the deck, where its life, of which it retained no symptoms, was despaired of by all.

The captain's humanity, if I may so call it, did not so totally destroy his philosophy, as to make him yield himself up to affliction on this melancholy occasion. Having felt his loss like a man, he resolved to shew he could bear it like one; and, having declared, he had rather have lost a cask of rum or brandy, betook himself to threshing at backgammon with the Portuguese friar, in which innocent amusement they had passed about two thirds of their time.

But, as I have, perhaps, a little too wantonly endeavoured to raise the tender passions of my readers, in this narrative, I should think myself unpardonable if I concluded it, without giving them the satisfaction of hearing that the kitten at last recovered, to the great joy of the good captain; but to the great disappointment of some of the sailors, who asserted that the drowning a cat was the very surest way of raising a favourable wind; a supposition of

which, though we have heard several plausible accounts, we
will not presume to assign the true original reason. **"**

ACCORDING TO BART

Stopping the boat might seem unusual to passengers, but it
was nothing out of the ordinary to the crew. Sailors regularly
fell or were knocked overboard and were hauled back on board
if humanly possible. The boatswain was probably the ship's
designated diver because he could swim and likely had saved
numerous lives over the years.

Imagine the headlines today. "Hero Sailor Braves Waves to Rescue Kitten" or "Sailor's Daring Dive to Rescue Kitten." A modern day Henry Fielding wouldn't wait to write a book; he'd video the whole event on his smartphone, post it to his Facebook page, and share it with the media. Instant front-page news around the world if he got a good shot.

"Sailor saves ship's cat" stories began to hit the headlines in the nineteenth century. Savvy editors found that they made good copy and sold papers. News about cats—cute or otherwise—has been fodder for *The New York Times* for more than 140 years, says University of Illinois journalism professor Matthew Ehrlich.

The stories began to appear in the 1870s, and increased during periods when the Times faced increased competition—in the 1920s from tabloids, in the 1970s from papers with new lifestyle and feature sections, and more recently from the Internet. In recent years, cat stories in the Times have averaged almost one a week, [Ehrlich] said.

Writers of cat stories have been known to stretch the truth or take complete liberties with it. Back in 1913, Ralph Pulitzer became so concerned about the increasing blurriness between "that which is true and that which is false" in his *New York World* that he set up the Bureau of Accuracy and Fair Play. Turns out one of the questionable practices his new bureau uncovered was the routine embellishment of shipwreck stories with reports about rescuing a ship's cat.

The bureau's director was curious why a cat had been rescued in each of a half dozen accounts of shipwrecks.

> One of those wrecked ships carried a cat, and the crew went back to save it. I made the cat the feature of my story, while the other reporters failed to mention the cat, and were called down by their city editors for being beaten. The next time there was a shipwreck there was no cat; but the other ship news reporters did not wish to take chances, and put the cat in. I wrote a true report, leaving out the cat, and then I was severely chided for being beaten. Now when there is a shipwreck all of us always put in a cat.

There's nothing new about fake news.

Incidentally . . .

Cats can swim but tend not to unless absolutely necessary, because getting wet is a problem—water soaks through both their top coat and undercoat, taking hours to lick dry. The renowned swimming cat, the Turkish Van cat, doesn't mind getting wet because it doesn't have an undercoat, and its top coat is moisture-resistant.

Swimming is something most land mammals can do instinctively, though it's more a dog paddle than anything you'd see at the Olympics. Extant apes are the exceptions to the rule—gibbons, orangutans, gorillas, chimps, bonobos, and *sapiens* all need to learn to swim.

Epitaph

"Matthew Flinders' Biographical Tribute to His Cat Trim"
Matthew Flinders, 1809

" To the memory of Trim,
the best and most illustrious of his race,
the most affectionate of friends,
faithful of servants,
and best of creatures.
He made the tour of the globe,
and a voyage to Australia, which he circumnavigated,
and was ever the delight and pleasure of his fellow
    voyagers.
Returning to Europe in 1803, he was shipwrecked in the
    Great Equinoxial Ocean;
This danger escaped, he sought refuge and assistance at
    the Isle of France,
where he was made prisoner, contrary to the laws of
    Justice, of Humanity, and of French National Faith;

and where alas! he terminated his useful career, by an
untimely death, being devoured by the Catophagi of
that island.
Many a time have I beheld his little merriments with
delight, and his superior intelligence with surprise:
Never will his like be seen again!
Trim was born in the Southern Indian Ocean, in the
year 1799, and perished as above at the Isle of France
in 1804.

Peace be to his shade, and Honour to his memory. "

ACCORDING TO BART

Matthew Flinders ("the man behind the map of Australia," as
historian Gillian Dooley puts it) was lost for words when Trim
disappeared. Not surprising if you've read his *Biographical Tribute
to the Memory of Trim*. It's one of the all-time great seafurring stories. They spent a lot of time together, they went through a lot
together, and they achieved a lot together charting Australia's
coastline. Then someone snatched Trim, his loyal shipmate. A
couple of options with this: fall apart or rise above. Trim
would have been proud to see Flinders rise above . . . it's what

he would have done: gone aloft, as he always liked to do (see
"Away Up Aloft!" on page 85).

Penguin Buddies

*"Journal of a Voyage Kept on Board Brig 'Cora' of
Liverpool Bound to New South Shetland"*
Captain Robert Fildes, 1820–1821

" [January 1821] After the loss of the *Cora* a tent was constructed of sails and other materials the great part of which consisted of 4 lines of puncheons in form of a square, the heads of the inside ones being taken out so that two men could stand in and sleep, both warm and dry, one of these which was to spare was taken possession of by the Cat, and two Penguins one day came up out of the water and took up their stations alongside of her in the cask, they neither minding the people in the tent or the Cat, nor the Cat them.

Poor shipwrecked puss used to sit purring alongside them apparently comfortable and pleased with their company. These penguins used to go to sea for hours and as soon as landed again would make direct for the tent and get into the cask. The crew would sometimes to plague them endeavour to keep them out by keeping the tent shut but they always found a way to get in by getting under the canvas. In this manner did they stop with us until we left the coast.

"

🐈 **ACCORDING TO BART**

No surprise that puss purred when the penguins dropped by—it was a bit of company. Fildes was no fun, shooting out of bed at the crack of dawn and heading off mapping and charting and place naming; and the beach was no place to be, completely taken over by sealers plying their ghastly trade. So "poor shipwrecked puss" was stuck in a tub in a tent on Desolation Island in the South Shetlands day in, day out.

"No human can survive alone in the Antarctic, and one's companions in that hostile continent become lifelong friends," writes biology professor David Campbell in his award-winning *The Crystal Desert*, an account of three summers he spent in the maritime Antarctic. The same goes for seafurrers. But puss was at a disadvantage in this hostile environment, being the only one of his kind on Desolation Island and possibly the first puss to ever set paw on its shore. A couple of friendly penguins must have provided light relief.

Who knows why the penguins dropped by? It's possible that what the *Cora*'s crew thought was just a pile of stones and a good place to pitch a tent wasn't "unoccupied territory" but the penguins' perennial breeding ground—these birds are deeply attached to their annual nesting site and their stones.

I asked Campbell what kind of penguins he thought they were. "One can only speculate," he said in an email, but "chances are overwhelming that they were brushtails: chinstrap, Adelie or Gentoo. If the event took place today I'd say chinstrap. They were the most abundant penguin when I visited the island in 2010. However, we can't use current abundances of these species to guide us in 1821, before whaling, before sealing, and before climate change."

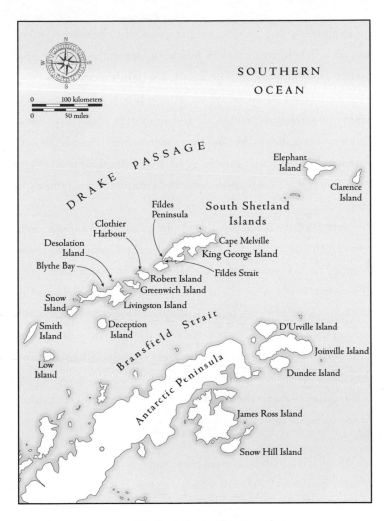

The South Shetland Islands

Explorers didn't come across penguins very often until sealers and whalers ventured into the Southern Ocean. Joseph Herring, mate on the *Williams* when the South Shetlands were discovered, hadn't seen one. In his rather unreliable July 3, 1820, account of events, he apparently said they found among the rocks "a species of very large bird, such as they had never seen before. These birds were so tame, that they sometimes dragged them from their nests; but to these they instantly returned, even while the men were standing by their sides."

Vasco Da Gama's was possibly the first European expedition to record seeing penguins. His ships rounded the Cape of Good Hope, dropped anchor near what's now Mossel Bay in South Africa, and discovered "birds as big as ducks, but they cannot fly and bray like donkeys" (November 25, 1497). It's likely Bartolomeu Dias had also spotted them there ten years earlier but didn't make a diary note. The locals, of course, would have been very familiar with penguins; they just didn't write about them.

Magellan's lot were the first Europeans reported to eat penguins. Antonio Pigafetta wrote:

We found two islands full of geese and goslings [penguins], and sea wolves [sea lions], of which geese the large number could not be reckoned; for we loaded all the five ships with them in an hour. These geese are black, and have their feathers all over the body of the same size and shape, and they do not fly, and live upon fish; and they were so fat that they did not pluck them, but skinned them. They have beaks like that of a crow.

For centuries, these "geese" were a bit of a mystery for *sapiens*. Initially they confused them with the great auk, a now-extinct large flightless bird with black and white plumage that was called "penguin."

Why *penguin*? It may be from the Welsh *pengwyn*, meaning "white head," posits the *Oxford English Dictionary*, and they back this up with the first written citation: "'Infinite were the Numbers of the foule, wch the Welsh men name Pengwin & Maglanus tearmed them Geese [sic]' (Francis Drake, *Golden Hind* log, Magellan Strait, 1577)." Penguins they remain.

Post-Darwin, *sapiens* mistook flightlessness for primitiveness and jumped to the conclusion that penguins were a missing link between dinosaurs and birds. Wrong. "Hardly primitive," said Campbell in *The Crystal Desert*.

Penguins are recent descendants of flighted birds, probably coast-dwelling relatives of petrels that took to sea about 40 million years ago, after Antarctica had split from the northern continents and became isolated in the Southern Ocean. As Antarctica slowly drifted south and became ice-locked, its resident penguins adapted to the increasingly hostile conditions. The penguins invaded a niche—the open and highly productive sea to a depth of several hundred meters—that was out of reach of all other birds. The evolution from flight to swimming involved a striking reversal of several adaptations that characterize flighted birds. Penguins lost their hollow, air-filled bones and evolved solid, ballasted ones. The wing bones, which in flighted birds are so adroitly and flexibly articulated, are in the aquatic penguin fused into a stiff flipper, a rudder-wing that is rigid enough to push through the heavy medium of water. In contrast to all other birds, their wings are designed to push down, not up; when they stop beating their wings, penguins bob upward and crash on the surface. Indeed, to say penguins are "flightless" is misleading, for penguins do fly on their modified wings, only their medium is water, not air.

Incidentally . . .

puncheon. n. large cask or barrel for liquids or other commodities, holding from 72 to 120 gallons.

All kudos to the Celts, who crafted watertight oak barrels to withstand stress (from rolling) and weight (from stacking) for transporting wine and other fermented beverages on their carts and boats. Much like container shipping, barrels were a turning point. Before long they were being used to store and ship just about everything from precious metals, powders, ochre, and sulfur to fish, olives, jam, mustard, vinegar, and pickled foods.

Ghost Ship

"A Ship Deserted"
Sailors' Magazine, *December 1840*

" A letter from Nassau, in the Bahamas, bearing date the 27th of August, has the following narrative:—'A singular fact has taken place within the last few days. A large French vessel, bound from Hamburgh to the Havannah, was met by one of our small coasters, and was discovered to be completely abandoned. The greater part of her sails were set, and she did not appear to have sustained any damage. The cargo, composed of wines, fruits, silks, &c., was of very considerable value, and was in a most perfect condition. The captain's papers were all secure in their proper place. The soundings gave three feet of water in the hold, but there was no leak whatever. The only living beings found on board were a cat, some fowls, and several canaries, half dead with hunger. The cabins of the officers and passengers were very elegantly furnished, and every thing indicated that they had been only recently deserted. In one of them were found several articles belonging to a ladies' toilet, together with a quantity of ladies' wearing apparel thrown hastily aside, but not a human being was to be found on board. The vessel, which must have been left within a very few hours, contained several bales of goods, addressed to different merchants in Havannah. She is very large, recently built, and called the Rosalie. Of her crew no intelligence has been received.'

"

ACCORDING TO BART

The real mystery is, who posted the letter? *Rosalie* wasn't a ghost ship—she seems to have been an imaginary ship. "I regret," reported Lloyds to a 1973 inquiry, "that a search of Lloyd's Records has failed to reveal mention of any incident involving a vessel named *Rosalie* in the Bahamas in 1840."

There was nothing imaginary, however, about the *Carroll A. Deering*, which foundered on Diamond Shoals, off Cape Hatteras, in 1921. It's a complete mystery and a cold case to this day, despite six departments of the US government, including the FBI, investigating. No wonder the conspiracy theorists and psychics have had a field day. Of her crew, no intelligence has been received, not even extraterrestrial or through-the-veil visitations.

The last man to see them alive was Captain Thomas Jacobson on North Carolina's Cape Lookout Shoals Lightship. He says on

January 29, an unidentified crewman on the *Carroll A. Deering* hailed him and reported they had lost their anchors. He later added that the crew seemed to be "scattered in an undisciplined fashion about the deck, particularly about the quarterdeck—the captain's province, his and his alone, sacrosanct."

Next sighting was January 31. Surfman C. P. Brady of the Cape Hatteras Coast Guard Station Number 183 spotted a schooner driven high on the shoals, but heavy seas made it impossible to get to the wreck. They telegraphed headquarters:

COAST GUARD WASHINGTON D.C.

UNKNOWN FIVE MASTED SCHOONER STRANDED DIAMOND SHOALS SAILS SET BOATS GONE NO SIGNS OF LIFE SEA ROUGH STATIONS NUMBER 183 184 186 UNABLE TO BOARD SCHOONER 1630

SEVENTH DIST.

No one could board until February 4, when the crew of salvage boat *Rescue* found a deserted ship—no anchors; no boats; smashed steering wheel and gear; burned-out running and distress lights; and no nautical instruments, no chronometer, no papers, and no ship's log. But there were clearly plans for dinner with a pot of pea soup, a pan of spareribs, and a pot of coffee on the stove.

"Yes, I was here when the *Carroll A. Deering* went on the point," recalled Doc Folb fifty years later:

She went with all five masts; all sails set. When the Coast Guard went out to her they found the table set. They never found a man, a boat, or anything. . . . I believe that the men got in the quicksand—it was awful quicksandy out there. Never found hide or hair, nor a boat or anything from her. Everything disappeared. The only survivor was a cat, I believe.

In fact, three cats were rescued and given a new home with the salvage boat's steward, L. K. Smith. Perhaps they continued seafurring with him, but it wouldn't be too surprising if they opted for terra firma.

Incidentally . . .

For every real ghost ship or derelict found adrift with crew and passengers inexplicably missing or dead like the *Carroll A. Deering*, there are countless legendary phantoms like the *Flying Dutchman*. Truth can be stranger than fiction at sea, but sometimes it turns out to be fiction after all.

Cannon Cat Cold Case

"The Loss of the **Monitor,** *by a Survivor"*
***Francis B. Butts,* Century Illustrated Monthly Magazine,**
December 1885

" Bailing was now resumed. I occupied the turret all alone,
and passed buckets from the lower hatchway to the man
on the top of the turret. I took off my coat—one that I had
received from home only a few days before (I could not
feel that our noble little ship was yet lost)—and rolling it
up with my boots, drew the tampion from one of the
guns, placed them inside, and replaced the tampion. A
black cat was sitting on the breech of one of the guns,
howling one of those hoarse and solemn tunes which no
one can appreciate who is not filled with the superstitions
which I had been taught by the sailors, who are always
afraid to kill a cat. I would almost as soon have touched a
ghost, but I caught her, and placing her in another gun,
replaced the wad and tampion; but I could still hear that
distressing howl. As I raised my last bucket to the upper

hatchway no one was there to take it. I scrambled up the ladder and found that we below had been deserted. I shouted to those on the berth-deck, 'Come up; the officers have left the ship, and a boat is alongside.'

"

Francis B. Butts was but a lad of eighteen learning the ropes as a landsman on the *Monitor* when he made his escape—he had joined up just a month before. He must have told his tale countless times to family and friends, trying out various embellishments before putting pen to paper for his presentation on the Civil War Battle of Hampton Roads and the sinking of the *Monitor* to the Rhode Island Soldiers and Sailors Society in 1878, which was later printed in *Century Illustrated Monthly Magazine*.

No self-respecting sailor lets facts get in the way of a good story. Mr. Butts' has all the signs of a well-practiced yarn spun for an appreciative (but not fainthearted) audience. The question remains: Did the USS *Monitor*, the first ironclad warship commissioned by the Union Navy during the Civil War, have an able-bodied seafurrer on board? No accounts actually written at the time mentioned one. Butts' account was published more than twenty years later. There were certainly rats on board. And over the summer of 1862, a portion of the iron deck was "converted into a stockyard containing just at present, one homesick lamb, one tough combative old ram, a consumptive calf, one fine lean swine, an antediluvian rooster & his mate, an old antiquated setting hen," according to Paymaster William Keeler—a very reliable witness—writing to his wife. So why not a cat?

It's highly likely there was a ship's cat. Just not the wet, very agitated, but seemingly compliant black one that didn't object to Mr. Butts singlehandedly stuffing it into a cannon with an eleven-inch opening on a dark and stormy night on a sinking ship.

Cold cases warm up when new furrensic evidence surfaces to sift through. In this case, what sank did surface in 2002, when the *Monitor*'s 120-ton rotating turret, which housed its two eleven-inch-bore cannons, was hoisted from its mid-Atlantic resting place. So this became an ongoing investigation, and researchers can look down the barrel. The reveal comes in a personal communication from marine historian Anna Holloway, formerly curator of the USS *Monitor* Center at the Mariners' Museum in Newport News, Virginia, for fourteen years before heading over to the National Parks Service and then SEARCH, Inc.

> Even with just one account, we had to approach the excavation of the turret and guns with the knowledge not only that there might be human remains there (16 men went down with the vessel, and in fact, we found two sets of human remains in the turret), but there might also be a cat, boots and a coat (along with other personal artifacts). We did discover a wool sack coat and one full boot in the turret—though not in one of the guns. The tompions for both guns were not evident. Still, we excavated the bores of both guns quite carefully. No kitty cat has been found so far—either in the turret or in the guns. There is still a small amount of concretion in the guns back at the breech—so

I suppose there is still a minuscule chance that cat bones could be found. So we keep looking because there's nothing ironclad about this case yet.

Incidentally . . .

USS *Monitor* broke the battleship mold forever.

- She was revolutionary, made of iron, not wood, and powered by steam and steam alone—no masts or sails.
- She was a radical departure from traditional design; barely a foot of her deck was visible because all machinery, storage, working, and berthing areas were below the waterline.
- She was heavily armored with an armor belt 5 feet (1.5 meters) high and 6 inches (15 centimeters) thick at the waterline, and had a revolving turret that was 9 feet (2.75 meters) high and 22 feet (6.7 meters) in diameter, and housed two 11-inch (279-millimeter) Dahlgren smoothbore cannons.

Less than two months after launching, she encountered the larger and more heavily armed Confederate *Virginia* in the Battle of Hampton Roads. They were the first iron ships to clash in naval warfare, signaling the end of wooden warships. But her end was nigh, too, because she wasn't very seaworthy. Shortly after midnight on December 31, 1862, while being towed by USS *Rhode Island* to Beaufort, North Carolina,

---

Monitor sank in a gale off Cape Hatteras. Her resting place, a mystery for more than a century, was found by scientists on Duke University's research vessel *Eastward* in August 1973. Her final resting place was designated the United States' first national marine sanctuary in 1975.

Soggy, Groggy Moggies

"Cat Overboard"
Newcastle Morning Herald and Miners' Advocate *(Australia),*
September 7, 1929

" This is the story of Tim, the ship's cat, of the Grimsby
steam trawler, Witham. Whilst Tim was running along
the ship's rail, out in the North Sea, a huge wave engulfed
the trawler, and swept the cat overboard. At once the
alarm was raised, and Skipper Howard brought the vessel
about, the crew springing to their stations as though the
alarm had been 'Man overboard.' Baskets and boards
were flung over the side to the struggling cat, who, paddling like a dog, was making a brave effort to keep his
head above water. Fifteen minutes elapsed before the vessel, hampered by her fishing gear, could be manoeuvred
into a position from which a basket, secured to a boat-
hook, could be extended to Tim, who, making a last
effort, drove his claws into the wicker work and held on
grimly until he was dragged on deck. Tim was for three

hours too exhausted to move, but later he recovered completely. The manoeuvre of the Witham was seen by a Dutch trawler, whose master assumed that a man had fallen overboard. He hurried at full speed to the spot, and was speechless with amazement, when he learnt the cause of the excitement. 〝

Scott's Last Expedition, Volume II
"Voyages of the Terra Nova *by Commanders E. R. G. R. Evans and H. L. L. Pennell"*
Second Voyage, Dec. 24, 1911

〝 The Sunday before Christmas, just as we were going to lunch, . . . the cat [who overindulged in moths and thus slept through the admiral's inspection on page III] fell overboard. He had been baiting the dogs on the poop, got uncomfortably close to one and, jumping to avoid the dog, went overboard. Fortunately it was an exceptionally calm day; the sea boat was lowered, and [he] was picked up and the ship on her course again twelve minutes after the accident. He was quite benumbed with the cold, but was taken down to the engine-room and well dried, given a little brandy to drink, and by the evening was all right again. 〝

 **ACCORDING TO BART**

Getting soggy is an occupational hazard not only for sailors but also for seafurring moggies (an affectionate British term for cats, possibly derived from Maggie, Margie, or Mog, short forms of Margaret). Aloft one moment, the ship rolls, in the drink the next. Trim regularly took a dive, said Matthew Flinders, because "the energy and elasticity of his movements sometimes carried him so far beyond his mark that he fell overboard."

Ships' cats needed all nine proverbial lives at their disposal. *The Book of Cats* author Charles H. Ross retold the tale of a black cat who first lost her tail when a squall came up, then not long after nearly lost her life:

> In Sydney we had hauled out from Campbell's Wharf to the stream, previous to sailing next day for England, and found, when the men had gone to bed, that the tailless black Cat was missing. It could not be below, as the hatches were battened down. About 3 A.M. next morning, the two men who kept anchor watch heard a piteous cry at the bows, and looking over saw a black object clinging to the chain cable, trying to get in at the hawse-pipe. One of them lowered himself down by a bowline, and handed up poor Pussy in an awful plight. She had swum off to the ship,—about three hundred yards. It took three or four days of nursing before

she recovered, but she got round at last, and remained in the ship for more than five years afterwards.

Resilient.

Seafurrers who have survived say that paddling around in the ocean trying to get their bearings, find the ship, and keep their head above water is hard work—that goes for sailors, too. But rescuing isn't a piece of cake. The skipper has to stop the ship and find them. "It seemed utterly impossible to find a tiny cat in all that waste of water, for the ship, even hove-to, was still drifting, and the cat was so small," reported Alan Villiers in *The Cruise of the Conrad* (1937) when their kitten Joseph fell overboard:

> The last glimpse I had had of poor Joseph was when an inquiring albatross, which had been gliding round, came down near him to examine this strange object, but the cat lifted a ginger paw and smote his visitor heartily over the nose, whereupon the startled albatross at once took off again and left him alone. The beak of an albatross would have made short work of poor Joseph! He knew that; but he was not one to be afraid. I could not leave a cat like that to drown.

In this case, puss is rescued and revived with "the help of the galley stove and a tot of rum" despite being in a bad way. The big

problem (for sailors and seafurrers) is hypothermia. Warm clothing and warm drinks are needed, but not alcohol, although that's probably what the rescuers felt like having after their valiant efforts. For felines, alcohol is absolutely off the menu. It's the ethanol—a killer. A little warm bone broth or fish stock will do the trick.

Incidentally . . .

Cats, and especially kittens, can get cold very quickly, even if we're not wet—frosty weather doesn't help on land or at sea. I asked Radio Pet Lady Tracie Hotchner for her tips on what a human needs to do to warm up a cold cat:

You can warm a cat by putting some towels in the dryer for a minute and then wrapping them up in them while taking them to the vet to be evaluated. Just as with people, do not rub a cat anywhere you suspect frostbite, since the friction can cause damage to their skin.

Hardtack Saves the Day

"Sailor Tells How Ship's Cat Rescued"
San Bernardino Sun *(San Bernardino, California)*,
July 3, 1942

> A GULF COAST PORT, July 2.—A 17-year-old Massachusetts seaman came back from his first torpedoing with the story of the ship's cat, which he saved.
>
> 'We were in the lifeboat seven and a half days with not much to eat besides hardtack,' he said. 'The cat didn't like hardtack, and wouldn't eat a bite until some flying fish landed in the boat. Before we got to shore, though, she ate hardtack and liked it.'

 **ACCORDING TO BART**

When it's hardtack or hunger and you are bobbing about in the Atlantic waiting to be rescued, saying, "No thanks, I'm paleo," or asking, "Is it gluten free?" is not a smart move in the survivor stakes.

Hardtack has a long history. It was the staple that sustained sailors. In 1190 Richard the Lionheart stocked his ships for the Third Crusade (1189–92) with "biskit of muslin" (mixed cornmeal made of barley, rye, and bean flour). He probably wasn't the first to do so but was just doing what everyone did back then to prepare for a long voyage. And he wasn't the last. Until steam-powered steel ships and galleys with baking ovens, hardtack was a sailor's daily bread. Samuel Pepys' 1677 table of Royal Navy rations allowed each sailor "one pound daily of good, clean, sweet, sound, well-baked and well-conditioned wheaten biscuit (plus a galleon of beer and other victuals)." Weevils were the protein bonus.

It was a molar breaker on its own, so it was often dunked in water or other liquid or added to salt beef stew or a seafood chowder, which made it easier to eat. The lifeboat lad possibly improvised a grainy seafood salad to tempt puss's taste buds (and his own) by tossing crumbled hardtack with fresh flying fish flakes moistened with a little water.

Hardtack not only saved seafarers and seafurrers; in 1835 it helped save a ship. The Portsmouth memorial for HMS *Pique* should read: "But for this stone *and a sack of ship's biscuit swollen with seawater* acting as a plug to one of the larger holes, she would certainly have foundered." But that's the way with historical objects. People collect rocks, not biscuits. They probably threw those out. Or ate them. The plaque instead reads:

> This stone was found wedged in a hole in the bottom of the Frigate H.M.S. PIQUE, (c/o Captain the Hon. H.J. Rous, R.N.) when the ship was docked in Portsmouth in October 1835. The PIQUE, had run ashore in the Belle Isle Straits, Labrador, in Sept. of that year. After refloating herself, she sailed across the Atlantic, without a rudder & with pumps continuously manned to control her leaks. But for this stone, acting as a plug to one of the larger holes, she would certainly have foundered. A splendid feat of seamanship.

Incidentally . . .

The Battle of the Atlantic was one of the longest campaigns of World War II. "The only thing that ever really frightened me during the war was the U-boat peril," Winston Churchill later said of the German U-boat threat to the Atlantic lifeline, the merchant ships from North America carrying food, raw materials (including oil), troops, and equipment to Britain. March 1943 was the month the Germans came close to overwhelming the convoys. Ninety British, Allied, and neutral ships were lost in the Atlantic.

Between 75,000 and 85,000 seamen lost their lives. Survivors had extraordinary tales to tell "of the smashed ships and the courage of the men who stood by," said Herbert Corey, reporting in March 1943:

> There was a ship's cat that thrust a distressed head through the glaze of fuel oil on the sea and looked at the men in a life boat. They were choking with oil. Blinded with it. The ship stumbled around on the sea. The men in the lifeboat slowly unshipped their oars and began to get her head around. The ship's cat watched them incredulously. When it was finally apparent that they were about to row away she opened her mouth.
>
> "Yaow," she cursed. "Yaow!"
>
> "B'jee," said an engineman. "The old lady's mad."

He fell into the water while they were getting her aboard. But they got her aboard. They slapped each other and laughed. Sailors are a hardy breed. Since the ship was still afloat, they boarded her again and found she might float.

MASCOTS

"STOWAWAY" JIM

CAME ON BOARD AT HALIFAX, N.S.
NOVᴿ 1914 - AND PASSED FOR "O.C." HE
HAS SINCE BEEN PROMOTED, AND
IS NOW C. IN C. OF THE P.R. CATS. HE
IS AN OLD WARDOG. AND BEARS
HIS BATTLE HONOURS "DOGGER-BANK"
AND "JUTLAND" UNOSTENTATIOUSLY.
"O.C." = ORDINARY CAT."

OUR MASCOT.

Stowaway Jim

WHISKIPEDIA

mascot: an animal, person, or thing that is sup-
posed to bring good luck

Mascot made its *Oxford English Dictionary* debut with Henry Brougham Farnie and Robert Reece's adaptation of Edmond Audran's opera comique *La Mascotte*, first performed at Brighton's Theatre Royal on September 19, 1881. "Ah! blest their lot whom fate shall send A true Mascotte, a fairy friend! Luck's his for ever!"

What a timely entrance. With military engagements on every continent apart from Antarctica in the first half of the twentieth century, the armed forces took to mascots big-time. It became common for cities and states with naval bases to present animals to the crew to wish them luck and show support for the military's efforts.

And it didn't take long for photographers on board to discover that seafurrers were very photogenic subjects. They certainly featured widely in publicity shots and news stories as ships' mascots with a key role to play. According to *The Photographed Cat*, mascots "were part of the team," providing service to the ship in their own way.

GUNNER AND GUNNERS MATES U.S.S. ALABAMA 1903

USS *Alabama*: Ship's Gunner and Gunner's Mates, 1903.
Note the kitten and parrot mascots.

The

FORECASTLE LOG

U. S. S. MEMPHIS

Santo Domingo City, D. R.
Puerto Plata, D. R.   **Monte Cristi, D. R.**

JUNE 3, 1916. Equipped ship's battalion in heavy marching order and made preparations for landing. The third, fourth and fifth companies of this ship's battalion left ship for duty in Santo Domingo City. Got underway at 11:05 p.m. for Puerto Plata, D. R. Received fourth, sixth, ninth and thirteenth companies of marines on board. *JUNE 4.* Held divine services on board. The Marines seemed to be well supplied with "Mascots" such as goats, dogs, cats and parrots. *JUNE 5.* At 6:59 a.m. came to anchor off Puerto Plata. At 12:11 p.m. the first steamer in returning to the ship, struck a reef and was sunk. Martin, D. (F1c) suffered contusion of the right shoulder. Sent wrecking party from ship to raise first steamer. Got underway at 9:38 p.m. for Monte Cristi, D. R. **Distance from Santo Domingo City to Puerto Plata 295 miles.** *JUNE 6.* At 6:30 a.m. anchored off Monte Cristi. At 7:45 a.m. received 13 bags of mail. Rigged ship for coaling. **Distance from Puerto Plata to Monte Cristi 69 miles.** *JUNE 7.* Commenced coaling at 5:30 a.m. and finished at 12:00 noon, having taken on 323 tons. At 1:33 p.m. got underway. At 6:20 p.m. stopped. At 6:36 p.m. got underway. *JUNE 8.* At 12:32 anchored off Puerto Plata. All hands engaged in raising first steamer. At 3:15 p.m. working party returned with starboard side of first steamer and engine. **Distance from Monte Cristi to Puerto Plata 319 miles.** *JUNE 9.* At 5:00 a.m. sent working party to recover boiler of first steamer. Recovered the boiler. Got underway for Santo Domingo City at 10:40 a.m.

USS *Memphis* Forecastle Log, June 3–9, 1916: "June 4. Held divine services on board. The Marines seemed to be well supplied with 'Mascots' such as goats, dogs, cats and parrots." Logs like this one were issued on Sundays as postcards that sailors could mail home to give their families an idea of where they were and what they (and their mascots) were up to. This, of course, was all before the US entered World War I on April 6, 1917.

Spick-and-Span

USS Maine, Berth Deck Cooks, 1896

 **ACCORDING TO BART**

These spick-and-span pots and pans are worthy of a prize. And it wouldn't be the first prize these deck cooks walked away with. Spearheaded by former plumbers Mario and Luigi (not identified in the photograph), the *Maine* mess crew took home the fleet's "Most Excellent Mustache" competition for three years in a row. They may well have gone on to greater mustachioed glory and made it a magnificent four, but a massive explosion onboard at 9:40 PM on the night of February 15, 1898, sent the *Maine* to the bottom of Havana Harbor, plunging the United States (eventually) into war with Spain and leading to its acquisition of Guam, Puerto Rico, the Philippines, and a naval base at Guantánamo Bay, and the building of the Panama Canal.

A spontaneous fire in a coal bunker that set off a nearby ammunition store was the likely cause. Others saw sabotage, blamed the Spanish, and agitated for retaliation. Front-page trumpeting in Joseph Pulitzer's *New York World* and William Randolph Hearst's *New York Journal* would give today's fake-news tweets an "alternative facts" run for their money.

More US naval personnel died in the *Maine* explosion than were killed during the entire Spanish-American War that followed. The *Maine*'s death toll? Two hundred and sixty men and two seafurrers, including the berth cooks' beloved mascot cat.

Tom, the ship's third seafurrer, survived and became a national hero among animal rights activists, who included Mrs. Charles Sigsbee, wife of *Maine*'s commanding officer. "Tom was wounded in one foot," she reported, "and was doubtless feeling very blue indeed, with his favorite sleeping-place destroyed, no friendly hands to minister to his wants, and nothing but ruin and water on every side!"

His savior was Commander Richard Wainwright, *Maine*'s executive officer (and great-great-grandson of Benjamin Franklin). He found Tom and took him to USS *Fern*, where he was treated for a wounded foot. Tom agreed to pose on a wicker armchair that had been salvaged from the *Maine* a few days later. It is reliably reported the photographer needed a whole fish to tempt him to stand on his sore paw.

Turning Tricks

"Mascots or Pets on Our Warships"
Wray Rattler (*Wray, Yuma County, Colorado*), April 21, 1911

" When a warship is engaged in an extensive cruise, the majority of the men aboard have, at one time or another, plenty of leisure at their disposal, and they devote a considerable portion of it to teaching tricks to the pets aboard. Many persons who have witnessed the really wonderful 'stunts' done by naval mascots or have noticed four-footed mascots marching in parade with a naval battalion, and conforming to all the military orders given, have gained the impression that the bluejackets possess an especial and almost unique knack for instructing dumb animals. The secret of their success, however, lies in the devotion of much time to the task, combined with the circumstances that the tars have a seemingly inexhaustible supply of patience and an almost unfailing fund of good humor, which, when reinforced by plentiful supplies of sweets, will ultimately win over the most stubborn furred or feathered captive.

One of the most remarkable tricks to the credit of any naval mascot is that of a famous cat that was domiciled aboard the cruiser Chicago a few years ago. This cat would sit on its hind legs and 'salute' with one front paw when the band played 'The Star-Spangled Banner,' and any person who knows how difficult it is to teach tricks to cats can appreciate what this performance meant.

ACCORDING TO BART

Getting the *Chicago's* cat to salute on cue is simply standard behaviorist training or operant conditioning—rewarding the desired behavior to encourage the animal (or person) to do it

again (and again). This is what animal trainers and pet owners have been doing for hundreds of years, long before B. F.
Skinner dipper-trained rats to press the right button to get
water (and not a shock).

The *Investigator* [*Spyall*] crew trained Trim enthusiastically, said
Matthew Flinders:

> His exercises commenced with acquiring the art of leaping
> over the hands; and as every man in the ship took pleasure
> in instructing him, he at length arrived to such a pitch of
> perfection that I am persuaded, had nature placed him in
> the empire of Lilliput, his merit would have promoted him
> to the first offices in the state.

"Leaping over the hands" is still a popular trick. It's not hard to
teach (or learn). It's done in easy stages with generous rewards along
the way. To get a seafurrer to jump like this on command, his shipmate first rewards him for walking over a stick lying on the ground,
and then for stepping over a slightly raised stick, and finally only
for jumps.

As for rewarding seafurrers for performing by having a plentiful supply of sweets, it's unlikely. Sea cats can't be bribed or rewarded with a sweet treat. However, a tasty meaty tidbit will do it. As will a nice piece of fish. It's said that the photographer had to give Tom—the only one of the *Maine*'s mascots who survived the 1898 explosion (see page 187)—a whole fish before he would stand properly for a photograph.

Why won't sweets work? Felines don't have a soft spot for things that taste sweet because our taste receptors can't detect sugar (big cats like tigers and cheetahs can't taste sweet, either). To get science-y, the taste receptor for sweetness is located in two genes that code for two proteins, both of which are involved in a human's ability to enjoy (and crave) sugary treats. In cats, a chance mutation appears to have broken one of these genes, and that's why lollies won't tempt them to leap through hooped hands.

Under Fire

"Cat Does Some High Jumping During Fight: Feline on Board English Armed Liner Badly Frightened by Noise of Big Guns"
Sacramento Union, January 4, 1915

" LONDON, Jan. 3.—During the fight in which the armed liner Carmania sank the German commerce destroyer Cap Trafalgar, the ship's cat on the Carmania broke various world's records in sprints and high jumps, writes a member of the crew to friends in London.

'The old cat didn't seem to know what to make of it,' says the letter. 'He was on ordinary occasions a lazy kind of a cat, and spent most of his time hunting sunny corners for sleep. But when the firing commenced, he covered the whole ship like a streak, from foc'sle head to stern, on deck and below, trying to climb masts and scramble up the funnel, and every time a gun was fired, he would jump up in the air as high as the tops of the freight booms. It was some time after the fight before he quieted down to his old habits. But we will match him

against any other cat in the world in his peculiar kind of athletics.'

""

 **ACCORDING TO BART**

This is the best of British humor—making light of grim business. Most likely the writer was trying to reassure the folks back home that he was OK. After all, he had just survived one of the earliest naval battles of the First World War. On September 14, 1914, the *Carmania* sank the *Cap Trafalgar*, but she didn't get off scot-free. She received seventy-nine hits and was badly damaged, her bridge wrecked and nine crew killed.

People react differently under fire, and so do animals. Some seem to be able to take it in their stride; for others, discretion is the much better part of valor. Gilbert Adshead, engine room artificer on HMS *Lord Nelson*, backed this up with personal experience. He reported:

> We had a black and a tabby cat. Now, the strange thing about the black cat was, gunfire never worried him a bit. He'd walk about on the top of a 12 inch turret when the 12 inch gun was firing. . . . His fur would stand right, completely up on end. He'd just look round and see what was happening, and never move. The tabby cat was terror-stricken. It was a long time before we found where he used to hide.

Navy ships had a lot of mascots in both world wars. Being good team players and natural morale boosters, seafurrers were probably the most popular, providing light relief and distraction. The cameras absolutely loved them, and they were frequently photographed in or on gun barrels, in their special hammocks, in or on hats, and at work or play and performing tricks.

Tudor Collins photographed this cat (detail) during the Second World War at Devonport Navy Base in New Zealand. No names, no dates, but the sailors were most likely the crew of a coastal mine sweeper.

Millions of animals were recruited in the First World War. Alan Taylor of the *Atlantic* explained why:

> When the war began, Europe's armies had an under-standing of warfare that put the use of cavalry in high regard. Soon, however, the deadly terrain that evolved around trench warfare rendered cavalry attacks nearly useless on the Western Front. But the need for constant resupply, movement of new heavy weaponry, and the transport of troops demanded horse power on a massive

scale—automobiles, tractors, and trucks were relatively new inventions and somewhat rare. British and French forces imported horses from colonies and allies around the world, a near-constant flow of hundreds of thousands of animals across the oceans, headed for war. One estimate places the number of horses killed during the four years of warfare at nearly 8 million. Other animals proved their usefulness as well: Dogs became messengers, sentries, rescuers, and small beasts of burden. Pigeons acted as messenger carriers, and even (experimentally) as aerial reconnaissance platforms. Mules and camels were drafted into use in various war theatres, and many soldiers brought along mascots to help boost morale. Only a couple of decades later, at the onset of World War II, most military tasks assigned to animals were done by machines, and warfare would never again rely so heavily on animal power.

First Aid

"Catnipped! The True Tale of Thomas Whiskers, USN"
Grog Ration, March–April 2008 (now the Grog)

" 13 December 1919
From: Commanding Officer, USS *Solace*
To: Commanding Officer, USS *Bell*
Subject: Ship's Cat

Several members of the crew of this ship have informed me the commanding officer that the mascot of the *Solace*, Thomas Whiskers, has been kidnapped or catnipped [sic] by certain members of your crew and is being impounded on board your ship. This mascot is a large, black Tom and when last seen was in dress uniform consisting of a leather collar with brass tag marked USS *Solace*.

If this cat is on board your ship, please inform me and I will send a member of the crew for it.

RWP

1920

From: Commanding Officer, USS *Bell*

To: Commanding Officer, USS *Solace*

Subject: Your letter of Dec. 13, 1919

Your ship's cat 'Whiskers' is being returned under guard, but an explanation of his presence aboard the ship is no doubt due you.

Prior to our departure from alongside the *Solace*, the cat in question developed a warm regard for the USS *Bell*, consequently spending much of his time aboard. On the morning we shifted berth his presence aboard was unknown to us. Later in the day after your ship had sailed, he was found to have taken possession of an unoccupied stateroom. The master-at-arms immediately made him prisoner on the ground that he was a stowaway and incarcerated him in the paint locker. This will account for the fact that he is no longer the black cat you describe, but battleship grey.

We advise against the removal of this collar since its low visibility aids the performance of his duties.

In regard to the dress uniform worn by the prisoner— in his attempts to remove the paint he pulled off the collar and lost it. This ship feels under no obligation in regard to the latter. In adding one ten cent collar to its stores it lost $2 worth of paint.

"

 **ACCORDING TO BART**

That really was the actual correspondence between the skippers of the hospital ship USS *Solace* and the destroyer USS *Bell*, regarding the disappearance of mascot Thomas Whiskers.

Solace was a hospital ship, so it's likely he played a key role providing comfort and cheer, perhaps speeding recovery by helping reduce stress. Pet therapy and companion animal research reports patients are happier, more alert and active, and less anxious when a pooch or a puss pops by.

Commissioned on April 14, 1898, for the Spanish-American War, *Solace* was one of the US Navy's first hospital ships and the first to fly the Red Cross, making it neutral under the terms of the 1864 Geneva Convention. At the time, the US Navy was very much in uncharted territory with hospital ships. With the exception of Civil War hospital ship USS *Red Rover* (1862–65), the US Navy did not operate a ship that was used solely for the purpose of tending to the sick and wounded and providing medical supplies. All that changed when the *Solace* came on the scene. US Navy Bureau of Medicine and Surgery medical historian André Sobocinski filled me in on the background:

> For the Spanish-American War, USS *Solace* was fitted to care for 200 patients comfortably (either in berths, swinging cots or staterooms). Her hospital was staffed by five medical officers, three hospital stewards, four mess men, and two laundry men. The ship carried steam launches and a barge for transferring the sick and wounded at sea, and had steam winches on both sides of its upper deck for the hoisting and lowering of the wounded. She would pick up her first patients (57 sailors and marines) on June 5 from ships that took part in the bombardment of San Juan, Puerto Rico. Among her many claims in the Spanish-American War was the first antiseptic surgery performed at sea.

She is the first of 20 Navy hospital ships to be blessed with a (daresay) soothing name. Originally known as the *Creole*—an ocean steamer from the Cromwell line—she was converted into a Navy hospital ship within 16 days. Her new name—USS *Solace*—was given to her by Margaret Long, the daughter of the Secretary of the Navy. Every US Navy hospital ship since 1898 has followed the *Solace*'s lead and been given a name denoting healing, peace, and refuge.

From 1908 to 1921, every ship captain was a medical officer. Usually ships are commanded by line officers. There were those in the Navy Medical Department who thought that hospital ships—as medical ships—should be commanded by physicians. While still president, Theodore Roosevelt agreed and directed that Navy medical officers be allowed to serve at the helm of hospital ships. Typically, since 1921, physicians and other medical-staff officers are able to serve as the Commander of the hospital or MTF (Military Treatment Facility) aboard the ship.

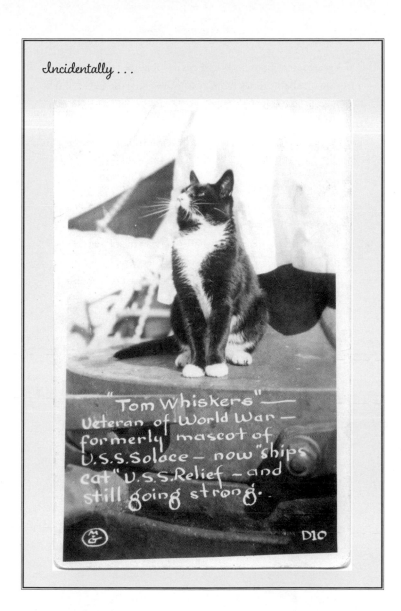

"Tom Whiskers" — Veteran of World War — formerly mascot of U.S.S. Solace — now "ship's cat" U.S.S. Relief — and still going strong.

A few years later, Thomas Whiskers was featured on a postcard. This one probably dates from 1921, says collector Brian Buckberry, as the *Relief*, the first US Navy ship designed and built from the keel up as a hospital ship, wasn't commissioned until December 28, 1920. In a personal communication, Brian shared a bit of postcard history:

> The beginning of the picture postcards that we know today is generally thought to be the early 1890s. Many references will point to the 1893 World's Exposition in Chicago as the start of picture postcards. They created numerous cards featuring scenes from the fair. The peak of the postcard collecting craze was around 1910 when the number of cards being traded around the world was phenomenal. That fortunately is the same time when the battleships became popular, so there are lots of early Navy postcards to be found. World War I set the postcard world back a bit because many of the best publishers of printed postcards were in Germany [a postcard of the *Chicago*'s cat saluting, story on page 189, was made in Germany]. But American, British, and French companies picked up the slack and continued making cards. Real photo postcards such as Tom Whiskers were popular from the early 1900s up to the 1940s. The 1930s–1940s saw the start of the "linen" postcards that have a texture to them, and the 1960s is when the "chrome" postcards that we know today were created.

The Real Deal,
or Tall Tale Deconstruction

"The Discovery's Mascot"
Brisbane Courier, September 30, 1931

" Among the vast miscellany of mascots given to various members of the recent Mawson expedition to the Antarctic was a suspicious looking bag, passed on board just as the Discovery was drawing away from the dock side at Capetown. The present bore a label: 'Open beyond three-mile limit.' The bag was passed below with a host of last-minute parcels, and forgotten, and it was not until the following day that a mewing coming from the bundles induced the bo's'n to make an investigation. Bo's'n Martin located the sound, which came from the suspicious bag, and on opening it a black kitten hopped out. . . . As the cat grew up she became a regular 'sea dog,' climbing aloft with the seamen, and venturing out on to the rocking yards. While navigating the ice-strewn seas, [she] slipped from the shrouds and fell into the sea. Martin saw the fall, and, rushing to the side, dived overboard to the rescue. It was some time before the vessel could be pulled up and a boat lowered. By the time this was done, Martin's strength began to give out and his muscles to contract with the icy cold. Both were rescued just in the nick of time. During the second voyage of the Discovery, . . . the alarm was given that there were four stowaways hidden beneath the boatswain's bunk, and on investigation four piebald kittens were discovered, which all survived. On the last stage of the voyage the Discovery encountered violent weather between Hobart and Melbourne, and one night [she] disappeared, being washed from the fo'castle head, while keeping watch with the bo's'n. ,,

ACCORDING TO BART

A shipping news reporter putting together a piece to entertain readers and get syndicated isn't going to be shy about a little embellishment. It's not "fake news"; it's harmless tall-tale fun. And there's a reasonable amount of fact in the fiction.

Not to let the cat out of the bag, but it is highly unlikely this ship's cat arrived gift wrapped (and silent!) in a suspicious bag with a label saying "Open beyond three-mile limit" in October 1929. However, she certainly arrived just before *Discovery* left Cape Town and was the

much loved and written-about mascot for both British Australian New Zealand Antarctic Research Expedition voyages in 1929–30 and 1930–31. It's not clear who had naming rights, but Sir Douglas Mawson always called her Blackie, as did a number of the scientists.

As for the account of the dramatic rescue, the cat wasn't "navigating the ice-strewn seas"; *Discovery* was stopped at the time, according to Captain Davis, and no boat was lowered. As Harold Fletcher told it, what actually happened is the stuff of a "get me outta here" reality show, where a lot of things go wrong before something goes right:

One of the crew happened to see Blackie, the ship's cat, jump from the gunwale into the sloping-out rubbish chute. Frantically clawing at the sides to save herself, she finally shot out into the sea. A cry of "cat overboard" brought all hands on deck and attempts were made to rescue Blackie as she swam alongside the drifting ship. Frustrated by the ineffectual efforts at rescue, Lofty Martin jumped overboard to save his pet, but the water was so cold he barely had time to tie a rope around his waist before succumbing to the cold. Dragged to the side, he was hauled on board half frozen, but soon recovered after a change of clothes and a good nip of rum provided by Captain Davis. In the meantime, Falla [the onboard ornithologist] had rescued Blackie by scooping her out of the water with a long-handled net.

In a follow-up radiogram, Sir Douglas Mawson clarified a number of things about what happened next, and what went before, which is what great leaders do:

This diversion did not affect Martin but the cat which was waterlogged was revived with great difficulty after many hours heating in the engine room. Blackie now quite restored will have no wish to essay world beyond ship.

Blackie had never been ashore, as very small kitten was transferred to Discovery at Cape Town Docks direct from research ship William Scoresby.

No surprise package.

Brush with Fame

Atlantic Conference August 1941,
War Office Second World War Official Collection,
photo by War Office official photographer

The official caption for this photo reads: "Churchill restrains 'Blackie' the cat, the mascot of HMS PRINCE OF WALES, from joining an American destroyer, while the ship's company stand to attention during the playing of the National Anthem." That's clearly not what's going on. No restraint. No one standing to attention. All eyes on the great man patting the cat minutes before one of the key events of the Second World War, the Atlantic Charter Conference—the first top-secret meeting between British prime minister Winston Churchill and US president Franklin D. Roosevelt, held off the coast of Newfoundland, August 9 to 12, 1941.

The War Office official photographer, Captain William Horton, deserves a big pat on the back for getting such a meaningful and informal shot when most mascot shots are posed. But Churchill was chided when the photograph published. Why? He patted the cat the wrong way, according to *Cat*, the monthly publication of the Cats' Protective League. *Cat* (or its editor) made the official pronouncement that cats abhor head patting, adding: "He should have conformed to the etiquette demanded by the occasion, offering his hand and then awaiting a sign of approval before taking liberties."

This must be up there with the all-time greats of petty remarks. Winston Churchill needed to go into that first meeting with FDR cool as the proverbial cucumber. There was a lot at stake at this point in the war. It's quite possible Blackie sensed this and reached out to the great man at this pivotal moment, thus playing a key role in contributing to the successful outcome of talks, where there would be some pretty tough bargaining. One of a seafurrer's regular jobs is to help keep things calm. Studies show that simply petting a cat raises the levels of three key chemicals in the human brain that help a person feel more relaxed—serotonin, dopamine, and oxytocin.

What happened next? Churchill and FDR came to terms, Blackie got a new name (Churchill), and HMS *Prince of Wales* steamed out to Singapore. On December 10, 1941, three days after their surprise military strike on the American naval base at Pearl Harbor, a strong force of Japanese high-level bombers and torpedo planes attacked and sank *Prince of Wales* along with HMS *Repulse*. More than 830 lives were lost. Churchill was among the survivors who made it to Singapore and safety, but he couldn't be found when orders came to evacuate Singapore two months later. The crew believed he had gone out hunting, but it's possible he decided it was time to disembark and stick with terra firma.

Incidentally . . .

The Atlantic Charter was negotiated at the Atlantic Conference (codenamed RIVIERA) by Winston Churchill and Franklin D. Roosevelt, aboard their respective war ships in a secure anchorage site just several hundred yards from land near a small community called Ship Harbour, Newfoundland. It was issued as a joint declaration on August 14, 1941, and is considered to be one of the key steps toward the establishment of the United Nations in 1945.

The opening paragraph reads:

> The President of the United States of America and the Prime Minister, Mr. Churchill, representing His Majesty's Government in the United Kingdom, being met together, deem it right to make known certain common principles in the national policies of their respective countries on which they base their hopes for a better future for the world.

The eight points are, in brief:

1. No territorial gains sought by the United States or the United Kingdom
2. Territorial adjustments must be in accord with the wishes of the people
3. The right to self-determination of peoples
4. Trade barriers lowered
5. Global economic cooperation and advancement of social welfare
6. Freedom from want and fear
7. Freedom of the seas
8. Disarmament of aggressor nations, postwar common disarmament.

The governments of Belgium, Czechoslovakia, Greece, Luxembourg, the Netherlands, Norway, Poland, Soviet Union, and Yugoslavia, and representatives of General Charles de Gaulle, leader of the Free French, unanimously adopted adherence to these common principles at the subsequent Inter-Allied Meeting in London on September 24, 1941.

Red Lead

Ship's Log, February 28, 1942

> Red Lead, ship's kitten, endeavoured to desert, but was brought back on board, despite vigorous protests.

Proud Echo
Ronald McKie, 1953

Perth was due to sail at 6 p.m., but delay in reassembling the native labour and disconnecting the fuel lines put sailing time back to 7 p.m. And that hour, which the Zero took from them, may have meant the difference between escape and destruction, between life and death for nearly two men in every three of that gallant company.

But something else happened that afternoon [February 28, 1942] which not one *Perth* survivor has forgotten. They talked about it in the mines of northern Japan, in Changi jail in Singapore, on the Burma railway, in the teak forests of Siam. They still talk about it when they meet, still shake their heads, for sailor superstition is strong and almost a religion of its own.

In *Perth* was a cat—a small black undistinguished cat not much older than a kitten. A girl gave him to one of *Perth*'s crew after a party on New Year's Eve, 1941, in Sydney. The sailor brought him aboard, where one of the first things he did was to upset a pot of red lead and christen himself to his own discomfort and the satisfaction of all. At this time *Perth* had a commander who disliked cats, and particularly disliked cats on His Majesty's Australian ships. So during daily rounds—that formal and terrifying walkabout commanders make—the sailors hid Red Lead in lockers, behind steam pipes, and even in kit bags. But keeping the cat quiet was not always easy, and one day a sailor had a brainwave. He decided that if Captain Waller approved their cat, then no commander, however prejudiced, would dare object, and Red Lead would be free to walk even the sacred quarterdeck without fear of being kicked overboard. But the sailor didn't ask the captain's permission to keep Red Lead.

He was much more subtle than that. He waited. And one day, when the word went through the grapevine that the captain was on the bridge, the sailor took the cat up topside and strategically released him. Red Lead did the rest. He seemed to know exactly what was expected of him. He wandered round the bridge, stropped himself against Waller's legs, and Waller picked him up and played with him. From that moment *Perth* would not have been *Perth* without her mascot. From that moment, too, Red Lead, with freedom from engine-room to turret, never attempted to leave the ship, but . . . That Saturday at Tanjong Priok Red Lead tried to escape. Three times he went down the gangway to the wharf and made for the godowns, and three times sailors chased him and brought him back. The news soon got about, and men shook their heads and began to remember other things, significant things, and with the superstition of men of the sea to add them up. "

ACCORDING TO BART

On February 28, 1942, HMAS *Perth* and USS *Houston* were making for the southern coast of Java after the fall of Singapore two weeks earlier. They were the only large Allied ships to have survived the Battle of the Java Sea the day before. Late that evening of the twenty-eighth, they encountered the Japanese western invasion convoy at the northern entrance to the Sunda Strait. Heavily outnumbered, *Perth* was sunk, as was *Houston*.

Of *Perth*'s ship's company of 681 men, 353 were lost during or just after the attack, along with Red Lead. Those who survived were gradually picked up by Japanese warships and became prisoners of war. They were held at first in Java, then sent north to work on the Burma-Thailand railway. Two hundred and eighteen men finally made it back home to Australia.

Of the 1,008 officers and men aboard USS *Houston*, approximately 350 escaped their sinking ship. Only 266 survived Japanese prisoner of war camps.

Disembarking

Statutory Instruments 1974 No. 2211
Animals—Diseases of Animals
The Rabies (Importation of Dogs, Cats and Other Mammals) Order
1974

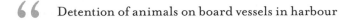 Detention of animals on board vessels in harbour

12.—(1) Subject to paragraph (2) below, it shall be the duty of the master of a vessel in harbour in Great Britain to ensure that an animal to which this Article applies—

(a) is at all times securely confined within an enclosed part of the vessel from which it cannot escape;

(b) does not come into contact with any other animal or any contact animal (other than an animal or contact animal with which it has been transported to Great Britain); and

(c) is in no circumstances permitted to land.

. . .

(5) The provisions of this Article shall apply to any animal which has, within the preceding six calendar months, been in a place outside Great Britain, Northern Ireland, the Republic of Ireland, the Channel Islands and the Isle of Man.

" "

🐈 ACCORDING TO BART

This may look like the end of a way of life at the stroke of a pen. But it had been in the cards for years with tougher quarantine regulations. As early as 1908, the UK Board of the Admiralty was insisting Board of Agriculture regs be strictly obeyed:

> In consequence of complaints made to the Board of Admiralty from the Board of Agriculture that goats, dogs, and other animals are brought to Great Britain from abroad in His Majesty's ships, and are detained on board for considerable periods, the Admiralty have issued a circular to commanding officers intimating that they are to discourage as far as possible the practice of bringing Home such pet animals from abroad on His Majesty's ships.

What happened next? Most seafurrers disembarked. Some disappeared dockside; others did time in quarantine and resettled on shore with old shipmates' families. A few lucky ones stayed on board, as the *Sun* reported in January 1976:

> A ship's cat has been saved from death by a special clause
> in a boat buying contract. Furness Withy, the British ship
> owners, insist that the Italian buyers should do their best
> to keep the Siamese cat Princess Truban Tao-Tai, happy
> in her old age. That means the cat, who has never left the
> 15,500-ton SAGAMORE since she joined the crew in 1959,
> will continue to have the run of the Captain's cabin. The
> Princess has travelled more than 1.5 million miles in the
> SAGAMORE and Furness Withy pleaded with the Italians
> not to have her put down. They eventually agreed. A Furness Withy spokesman said "She is coming to the twilight
> of her life now and we didn't want to see her destroyed."

Doors close. Doors open. The seafurrer's story has always been one of embracing change. There are still seafurrers. Now equipped with passports and vaccinations, they sail as shipmates to round-the-world sailors. But that's another tale for another chapter and another book.

Princess Truban Tao-Tai

Fear that rabies might cross the English Channel prompted this 1974 British order. Fox rabies was on the move. It first occurred in Poland in the 1940s, crossed Germany, and by 1969 was in eastern France. But it was the death from rabies of Fritz the terrier, which an army family brought back to the UK from Germany, that made it front-page news, precipitating panic, a government inquiry, and calls for tough measures.

Animal mascots remained on the British navy's ships until September 1977, when orders were issued to "land your warm-blooded animals forthwith," according to Michael Wynd, researcher at the National Museum of the Royal New Zealand Navy. "All mascots had to be removed by the beginning of October. The list of animals issued at the time included: otters, hyenas, lions, armadillos, elephants, apes, cats, dogs."

Acknowledgments

Embarking on a book is like embarking on a voyage—there's a lot of prep, and you can't do it on your own. Just as *sapiens* needed seafurrers to help them lap and map the world, this seafurrer needed *sapiens* to help research and write this book and is most grateful for their help. There are many to thank:

For staunch support and inspiring designs: Clare Forte and Ky Long

For boosting when all seemed becalmed: editor Bernadette Foley of Broadcast Books (broadcastbooks.com.au); illustrator Ad Long; and marketing guru Brett Osmond of Leading Hand Design (leadinghand.com.au)

For picture research: Walter Alvarez, University of California, Berkeley, and Henrique Leitão, University of Lisbon; Brian Buckberry; Paul Restall, photographic archivist at the National Museum of the Royal New Zealand Navy; Kat Southwell and Susie Raymond, the Australian War Memorial; Inger Sheil, Australian National Maritime Museum; Neera Puttapipat, Imperial War Museum, London; and Emily Beech, National Maritime Museum, Greenwich

For leads, feedback, fact checking, or permission: Roy and Lesley Adkins; David Campbell, Grinnell College; Matthew Ehrlich,

University of Illinois; Frank Fish, West Chester University; Anna Holloway, maritime historian; David Hunt; Lisette Flinders Petrie and John Flinders; André B. Sobocinski, Communications Directorate Bureau of Medicine and Surgery, US Navy; James Delgado, maritime archaeologist, explorer, author; Gillian Dooley, honorary senior research fellow at Flinders University; Heather Farley, historian, US Coast Guard Historians Office; Peggy Gavan, *The Hatching Cat* (hatchingcatnyc.com); Richard King, research associate with Williams-Mystic; Iain McKie; Lindsey Shaw, navy curator; Cindy Vallar, pirate history buff (cindyvallar.com/pirates.html); John Weale, Montreal; and Michael Wynd, researcher, National Museum of the Royal New Zealand Navy

For freely accessible digitized newspaper resources: Trove (National Library of Australia) and California Digital Newspaper Collection

For creating this book: The Experiment Publishing team—Matthew Lore, publisher; Jeanne Tao, editor; Liana Willis, editorial assistant; Sarah Smith, art director; and Jennifer Hergenroeder, publicity and marketing director; as well as freelance copy editor Suzanne Fass and proofreader Sally Knapp

For maps: John Frith

For being a word detective: Alan Kirkness; and for translating: Alison Kirkness

For being there: Richard Sandall and Emma Sandall

For endless hours of chair warming: Silkie Sandall

Silkie Sandall

Permissions Acknowledgments

Every effort has been made to trace and contact copyright holders. If an error or omission is brought to our notice, we will be pleased to correct the situation in future editions of this book. For further information, please contact the publisher.

ILLUSTRATION CREDITS

Maps on pages 2, 23, 44, 81, and 155 copyright © 2018 by John Frith.

Ad's illustrations are cobbled together from his own photographs and drawings, and from clipped, flipped, and scribbled-on images in the public domain with no known restrictions on publication. Credit is due to the original photographers/artists/sources for the following images:

p. 62. The successful explorers at the South Pole (Roald Amundsen, Olav Olavson Bjaaland, Hilmer Hanssen, Sverre H. Hassel, and Oscar Wisting), December 17, 1911. Photo: Olav Bjaaland, courtesy of the National Library of Norway, commons.wikimedia.org/wiki/File:Amundsen_Expedition_at_South_Pole.jpg.

p. 79. William Dampier, a circa 1785 engraving by an unknown artist after a 1781 engraving by Charles Sherwin, which was in turn after a circa 1697 portrait by Thomas Murray.

p. 134. USS *Pawnee*. View on deck, looking aft from the forecastle, circa 1863–64. An "Old Salt" is standing by the ship's 100-pounder Parrott rifle, with the starboard battery of nine-inch Dahlgren shell guns visible beyond. From *Civil War Times Illustrated* magazine. US Naval Historical Center Photograph NH 61926.

p. 163. *Maipo*, State Library of Queensland, commons.wikimedia.org/wiki/File:StateLibQld_1_143171_Maipo_(ship).jpg.

p. 166. *James River, Va. Deck and turret of U.S.S. Monitor*. Gibson, James F., photographer. United States. July 1862, printed between 1890 and 1910. Retrieved from the Library of Congress, loc.gov/item/2011647352 (accessed September 26, 2017).

p. 193. The Brazilian Battleship *Minas Geraes* firing a broadside, 1909, during *Minas Geraes*' sea trials. Brazilian Navy (public domain), commons.wikimedia.org/wiki/File%3ABrazilian_battleship_Minas_Geraes_firing_a_broadside.jpg.

p. 207. *Endeavour* Replica rigging detail, commons.wikimedia.org/wiki/File:Endeavour_IB.jpg.

PHOTO CREDITS

p. iii. Sailor with pet cats sitting on hatch cover, Sydney, circa 1910: Image: Samuel Hood/Australian National Maritime Museum.

p. ix. Decorative column at Jéronimos Monastery: Courtesy of Richard Sandall.

p. x. A seaman enticing the ship's cat up one of the shrouds of *Pommern*. Circa 1931–32. © National Maritime Museum, Greenwich, London.

p. 8. The gun crew of HMAS *Sydney*'s port number 3 (P3) 6-inch gun: Australian War Memorial.

p. 72. Crew with Simon: Courtesy of PDSA (People's Dispensary for Sick Animals).

p. 91. *Ten "Old Salts"*: US Naval History and Heritage Command Photograph NH 63033.

p. 94. Tailors of USS *New York*: Edward H. Hart, photographer. Detroit Publishing Co., publisher. Retrieved from the Library of Congress, loc.gov/item/det1994014000/PP (accessed April 25, 2017).

p. 102. Drawing of Nansen by cabin boy Johan Koren: from Frederick Cook, *Through the First Antarctic Night, 1898–1899*, 1900.

p. 112. Six Bell Sleeper, mascot of USS *Wyoming*: Courtesy of Brian Buckberry.

p. 117. North Sea. Some Crew Members of Battlecruiser HMAS *Australia* (I): Black and white, glass original half plate negative, Naval Historical Collection, Australian War Memorial.

p. 120. The catering crew of SS *Newcastle*. Sydney, circa 1910–20: Image by Samuel Hood/Australian National Maritime Museum.

p. 181. Stowaway Jim: Courtesy of Brian Buckberry.

p. 183. USS *Alabama*: Ship's Gunner and Gunner's Mates, 1903: US Naval History and Heritage Command Photograph NH 57497.

p. 184. USS *Memphis* Forecastle Log, June 3–6, 1916: US Naval History and Heritage Command.

p. 185. USS *Maine*, Berth Deck Cooks, 1896: Edward H. Hart, photographer. Detroit Publishing Co., publisher. Retrieved from the Library of Congress, loc.gov/item/det1994010230/PP.

p. 195, 196. Tudor Collins photograph: National Museum of the Royal New Zealand Navy, Tudor Collins Collection.

p. 203. Thomas Whiskers postcard: Courtesy of Brian Buckberry.

p. 210. Atlantic Conference August 1941: Winston Churchill stops "Blackie," ship's cat of HMS *Prince of Wales*, crossing over to a US destroyer during the Atlantic Conference, August 1941. War Office Second World War Official Collection, Imperial War Museums. © IWM (H 12756).

p. 226. Silkie Sandall: Courtesy of Philippa Sandall.

p. 230. A cat sitting in the fairlead of the barque PAMIR (Sydney, Australia): Image by Samuel Hood/Australian National Maritime Museum.

PERMISSIONS ACKNOWLEDGMENTS

Notes

PREFACE

vii "to sail southwards": In Sonia E. Howe, *In Quest of Spices* (London: Herbert Jenkins, 1946), 90.

EMBARKING

4 "In seven houses there are seven cats": In Neil MacGregor, *A History of the World in 100 Objects* (New York: Viking, 2011), 103.

6 "so that you may open treasuries": Ibid., 107.

7 "the only speck of sentimental life": Frederick Cook, *Through the First Antarctic Night, 1898–1899: A Narrative of the Voyage of the "Belgica" Among Newly Discovered Lands and over an Unknown Sea About the South Pole* (London: William Heinemann, 1900), 326.

7–8 "the most repulsive of all creatures": Roald Amundsen, *The South Pole: An Account of the Norwegian Antarctic Expedition in the "Fram," 1910–1912*, trans. A. G. Chater, vol. 1 (London: John Murray, 1913), 61.

9 "Of all those [vermin] infesting ships": Robert White Stevens, *On the Stowage of Ships and Their Cargoes* (Plymouth: Stevens, 1858), 157.

MOUSERS AND MORE

11 "Tiger came aboard in Djibouti": In Martyn Lewis, *Cats in the News* (London: Macdonald Illustrated, 1991), 95.

12 "Owls . . . are counted": In *Oxford English Dictionary*, s.v. "Mouser," oed.com.

A ship's cat balances in a fairlead (opening in the ship's side for cable) high up the topsides of the *Pamir*, one of the last commercial sailing ships on world routes.

12 "He is the best Mouser that can be": John Lawson, *A New Voyage to Carolina: Containing the Exact Description and Natural History of that Country* (London: n.p., 1709), 132.

13 "to spend 1d [1 penny] a day": "Tale of Home Office Cat," *Metro*, January 4, 2005, metro.co.uk/2005/01/04/tale-of-home-office-cat-259530.

INCIDENT 1: DON'T FORGET THE CAT

14 "NOTE LVIII: If goods laden on board": Roccus (Francesco Rocco), *A Manual of Maritime Law: Consisting of a Treatise on Ships and Freight and a Treatise on Insurance*, trans. Joseph Reed Ingersoll (Philadelphia: Hopkins and Earle, 1809), 56–57.

15 "Through charity alone, with much labour": *The Monthly Anthology and Boston Review*, vol. 6 (Boston: Hastings, Etheridge and Bliss, 1809), 133.

16 "If the ship has had cats on board": In John Weale, "If a Ship Is Lost to a Peril of the Sea, How Can You Say She Was Seaworthy?" (unpublished paper provided by the author).

17 "a doge and a cat with all other necessaryes": In Dorothy Burwash, *English Merchant Shipping 1460–1540* (Toronto: University of Toronto Press, 1947), 40.

INCIDENT 2: SOUTH SEA ADVENTURES

18–19 "Heere we made also a survay": Richard Hawkins, *The Observations of Sir Richard Hawkins, Knt, in His Voyage into the South Sea in the Year 1593*, ed. C. R. Drinkwater Bethune (London: Hakluyt Society, 1847), 134–35.

20 "to make a perfect discovery": Ibid., 7.

21 "After going and taking the course": Antonio Pigafetta, *The First Voyage Around the World, by Magellan*, trans. Lord Stanley of Alderley (London: Hakluyt Society, 1874), 57.

24 "The Sweet potatoes are set out": James Cook, *The Journals of Captain James Cook on His Voyages of Discovery*, vol. 1, ed. J. C. Beaglehole (Cambridge: Cambridge University Press for the Hakluyt Society, 1968), 583–84.

24 "to attempt, with a ship, bark, and pinnace": Mary W. S. Hawkins, *Plymouth Armada Heroes: The Hawkins Family* (Plymouth: William Brendon and Son, 1888), 117.

INCIDENT 3: SURVIVOR

25–26 "He [Alexander Selkirk] had with him": Woodes Rogers, *A Cruising Voyage Round the World* (London: A. Bell, 1712), 126, 128.

27 "from a leaky Vessel": Richard Steele, "Alexander Selkirk," *Englishman*, at Alexander Selkirk (website), updated January 26, 2013, academic .brooklyn.cuny.edu/english/melani/novel 18c/defoe/selkirk .html#steele.

28 "Fish, particularly Snappers and Rock-fish": William Dampier, *A New Voyage Round the World*, vol. 1 (London: James Knapton, 1699), 88.

29 "He might have had Fish enough": Rogers, *A Cruising Voyage Round the World*, 126–27.

29–30 "This Indian lived here alone": Dampier, *A New Voyage Round the World*, 84–85.

INCIDENT 4: SAILING INTO HISTORY

31–32 "[1768—September] 28. Wind rather slackend": Joseph Banks, *The Endeavour Journal of Joseph Banks, August 1768–July 1771*, Papers of Sir Joseph Banks, State Library of New South Wales, www2.sl.nsw.gov.au/banks/ series_03/03_032.cfm.

34 "fine Library of Natural History": In L. A. Gilbert, s.v. "Banks, Sir Joseph (1743–1820)," *Australian Dictionary of Biography*, National Centre of Biography, Australian National University, adb.anu.edu.au/biography/ banks-sir-joseph-1737, published first in hard copy 1966.

35 "It was Banks who first recommended": David Hunt, *Girt: The Unauthorised History of Australia, Volume 1* (Carlton, Victoria: Black Inc., 2013), 51.

INCIDENT 5: BEATING SCURVY'S SCOURGE

36–37 "[Table Bay, Cape of Good Hope] On the 11th": John Rickman, *A Journal of Captain Cook's Last Voyage to the Pacific Ocean, on Discovery; Performed in the Years 1776, 1777, 1778, 1779* (London: E. Newbery, 1781), 18, 20–21.

37 "The Ship being a good [deal] pestered": In "225 Years Ago: October–December 1777," Captain Cook Society, captaincooksociety.com/home/ detail/225-years-ago-october-december-1777, originally published in *Cook's Log* 25, no. 4 (2002): 2011.

39 "their Superiors set a Value upon it": In Egon H. Kodicek and Frank G. Young, "Captain Cook and Scurvy," *Notes and Records of the Royal Society of London* 24, no. 1 (June 1969), 47.

39 "We were all hearty seamen": Ibid., 43.

INCIDENT 6: NAMING RIGHTS

41–42 "Feb. 21 [1842]: The southerly gale continued": James Clark Ross, *A Voyage of Discovery and Research in the Southern and Antarctic Regions, During the Years 1839–43*, vol. 2 (London: John Murray, 1847), 197–98.

42–43 "discovered a land of so extensive a coastline": In "Erebus and Terror—The Antarctic Expedition 1839–1843, James Clark Ross," Cool Antarctica, coolantarctica.com/Antarctica%20fact%20file/History/antarctic_ships/erebus_terror_antarctica.php.

45 "as far to the east and west": James Clark Ross, *A Voyage of Discovery and Research in the Southern and Antarctic Regions, During the Years 1839–43*, vol. 1 (London: John Murray, 1847), 232.

45–46 "Few people of the present day": Amundsen, *The South Pole*, 12.

INCIDENT 7: COLLECTOMANIA

47–50 "July 25 [1879].—During the morning": Morton MacMichael III, *A Landlubber's Log of His Voyage Around Cape Horn* (Philadephia: J. B. Lippincott and Co., 1883), 19–20, 54, 73–75.

51 "If I only knew how many teeth": In Julian Cribb, *Surviving the 21st Century: Humanity's Ten Great Challenges and How We Can Overcome Them* (Canberra: Springer, 2016), 7.

53 "Wee saw land againe lying north west": In Adrian Flanagan, *The Cape Horners' Club: Tales of Triumph and Disaster at the World's Most Feared Cape* (London: Bloomsbury, 2017), 97.

INCIDENT 9: WAR ON RATS

59 "We had a considerable collection": Amundsen, *The South Pole*, 61.

59–61 "Chapter XVI: The Voyage of the 'Fram'": Ibid., 325–27.

61–62 Naturalist Desmond Morris: Desmond Morris, *Catwatching: The Essential Guide to Cat Behaviour* (London: Ebury Press, 2002), 55.

64–65 Ethologist Paul Leyhausen: Paul Leyhausen, *Cat Behavior: The Predatory and Social Behavior of Domestic and Wild Cats*, trans. Barbara A. Tonkin (New York: Taylor & Francis/Garland STPM Press, 1979).

INCIDENT 10: CLASSIC CATCHES

68–69 "1768 September 25. Wind continued": Banks, *The Endeavour Journal of Joseph Banks*.

69–70 "To take to the air, a flying fish leaps": Frank Fish, "On a Fin and a Prayer," *Scholars* 3, no. 1 (Fall/Winter 1991–92): 5–6.

INCIDENT 11: FIRING LINE TO FAME

71 "Served on HMS Amethyst": "PDSA Dickin Medal for Gallantry," People's Dispensary for Sick Animals, pdsa.org.uk/what-we-do/animal-honours/the-dickin-medal.

73–74 "There were a large number of rats": In Nick Cooper, "Simon of the *Amethyst*," nickcooper.org.uk/moggies/simon/simon.htm.

MATES

76 "If Maizie [the ship's cat] hadn't been with us": "Maizie, the Seagoing Cat: Comforted 6 Seamen on Raft and Shared Their Rations," *Lookout* 43, no. 9 (September 1943): 10.

77 "Whence the saw: 'Messmate before a shipmate'": William Henry Smyth, *The Sailor's Word-Book* (London: Blackie and Son, 1867), 478.

INCIDENT 12: VITAL VICTUALS

78 "[Setting out from Cape Corrientes]": William Dampier, *A New Voyage Round the World* (London: Adam and Charles Black, 1937, from Dampier, 1697), Project Gutenberg Australia eBook, gutenberg.net.au/ebooks05/0500461h.html.

78–79 "There was not any occasion to call men to victuals": In Anton Gill, *The Devil's Mariner: A Life of William Dampier, Pirate and Explorer, 1651–1715* (London: Michael Joseph, 1997), 182.

80 "The 20th day of May": Dampier, *A New Voyage Round the World*, Project Gutenberg Australia eBook.

81 "impelled to adopt the horrible expedient": William Boys, *An Account of the Loss of the Luxborough Galley, by Fire, on Her Voyage from Jamaica to London*, quoted in Taylor Zajonc, "1727—Luxborough Galley," *Expedition Writer* (blog), July 2, 2014, expeditionwriter.com/1727-luxborough-galley.

82 "All cultures go to considerable lengths": Robin Fox, *The Challenge of Anthropology: Old Encounters and New Excursions* (New Brunswick, NJ: Transaction, 1995), 40.

82–83 "Wednesday, the twenty-eighth of November": Pigafetta, *The First Voyage Around the World*, 64–65.

83 "The Diligent [*La Diligence*] was full of rats": In Roy and Lesley Adkins, *Jack Tar: The Extraordinary Lives of Ordinary Seamen in Nelson's Navy* (London: Abacus, 2009), 72.

83–84 "Our ship was full of rats": James Anthony Gardner, *Recollections of James Anthony Gardner, Commander R. N. (1775–1814)*, ed. R. Vesey Hamilton and John Knox Laughton (England: Navy Records Society, 1906), 244–45.

INCIDENT 13: AWAY UP ALOFT!

85–86 "The replacing a top-mast": "Matthew Flinders' Biographical Tribute to His Cat Trim," The Flinders Papers, National Maritime Museum, flinders.rmg.co.uk/DisplayDocument0726.html?ID=92&CurrentPage=1&CurrentXMLPage=All.

88 "There is a tradition in Trinity": In Lewis Campbell and William Garnet, *The Life of James Clerk Maxwell* (London: Macmillan and Co., 1882), 499.

88 "the speed and agility with which a cat turns over": Donald McDonald, "How Does a Cat Fall on Its Feet?" *New Scientist*, June 30, 1960: 1649.

INCIDENT 14: TEAM PLAYERS

92–93 "he lectured to the men": Clifford M. Drury, *History of the Chaplain Corps, United States Navy*, vol. 1 (Washington, DC: Bureau of Navy Personnel, 1948), 126.

INCIDENT 15: ALL ABOARD

95 "Monday, December 23, 1895": Mark Twain, *Following the Equator: A Journey Around the World* (New York: Doubleday and McClure Co., 1897), 331.

97 "In 1819 a favourite Tabby": Charles H. Ross, *The Book of Cats* (London: Griffith and Farran, 1868), 126–27.

INCIDENT 16: THE CONSOLATION OF PETS

100–101 "June 26.—It is Sunday": Frederick Cook, *Through the First Antarctic Night, 1898–1899*, 325–26.

103 "PORT TOWNSEND. Nov. 27.": "Saved by a Cat from Drowning: Feline Pet Scratches the Face of a Sleeping Man on a Sinking Ship," *San Francisco Call* 84, no. 181, November 28, 1898.

103–4 "The sailors, particularly those on board": "Sailors' Pets," *People's Press* (Winston-Salem, NC), July 14, 1892.

INCIDENT 17: VIGILANCE

108–9 "Nine men of the crew": "Cat Saves Lives of Nine," *Healdsburg Tribune* (Healdsburg, CA), April 27, 1920.

INCIDENT 18: SLEEPING QUARTERS

110–11 "[Monday, October 17, 1910] The Admiral and his officers": Edward Wilson, *Diary of the Terra Nova Expedition to the Antarctic 1910–1912*, ed. H. G. R. King (London: Blandford Press, 1972), 55.

111 "not feeling very well, owing to the number of moths": Apsley Cherry-Garrard, *The Worst Journey in the World: With Scott in Antarctica 1910–1913* (Mineola, NY: Dover, 2013), 32.

112 "a great many Indians in canoes": Wikipedia, s.v. "Hammock," last modified November 26, 2017, 15:08, en.wikipedia.org/wiki/Hammock.

113–14 "Most people, I presume, know": Basil Hall, *Fragments of Voyages and Travels, Including Anecdotes of a Naval Life*, vol. 1 (Edinburgh: Robert Cadell, 1831), 248–49.

114–15 "The Indians sleep in a bed": In "What Came to Be Called America," *1492: An Ongoing Voyage*, Library of Congress exhibition, 1992–93, loc.gov/exhibits/1492/america.html.

115 "woven out of bark from a hamack tree": Wikipedia, "Hammock."

115 "The *Magurie*-Tree or *Cabuya*": Hans Sloane, *A Voyage to the Islands Madera, Barbados, Nieves, S. Christophers and Jamaica*, vol. 1 (London: B. M., 1707), 247.

INCIDENT 19: MATESHIP

119 "a pigeon; a couple of canaries": "Podcast 34: Animals in War," Imperial War Museums, iwm.org.uk/history/podcasts/voices-of-the-first-world-war/podcast-34-animals-in-war.

INCIDENT 20: JOBS FOR THE GIRLS

121 "Her cabins are spacious": In John Kennedy, *The History of Steam Navigation* (Liverpool: Charles Birchall, 1903), 14.

121 "Ladies will have a female steward": Sari Mäenpää, "Comfort and Guidance for Female Passengers: The Origins of Women's Employment on British Passenger Liners 1850–1914," *Journal for Maritime Research* 6, no. 1 (2004): 148.

122 "When the ship is lying at any foreign port": Ibid., 155.

122 "I am convinced that it is a very desirable thing": Ibid., 152.

123 "[October 16, 1876] . . . Some of the girls": Ibid., 153.

INCIDENT 21: ABLE-BODIED SEAFARING CAT WANTED

129 "there are few animals in whose faces": Konrad Lorenz, *Man Meets Dog* (London: Penguin, 1964), 175–76.

MISADVENTURES

130 "An extraordinary thing happened": In Caroline Alexander, "Mrs. Chippy, R.I.P.," *The New York Times*, November 21, 2004, nytimes.com.

INCIDENT 22: WRECK RIGHTS

132 "Concerning wreck of the sea": Lawrence J. Lipka, "Abandoned Property at Sea: Who Owns the Salvage 'Finds'?" *William and Mary Law Review* 12, no. 1 (1970): 99–100.

133 On just one day, December 5, 1388: In Tom Johnson, "Medieval Law and Materiality: Shipwrecks, Finders, and Property on the Suffolk Coast, ca. 1380–1410," *American Historical Review* 120, no. 2 (April 1, 2015): 407–32.

134–35 "Trim was undisputed master of them all": "Matthew Flinders' Biographical Tribute to His Cat Trim."

135 "A dog is the most obvious": Basil Hall, *Fragments of Voyages and Travels*, vol. 2 (Edinburgh: Robert Cadell, 1832), 112.

135–36 "I messed in the main hatchway berth on the lower deck": Gardner, *Recollections of James Anthony Gardner*, 47.

INCIDENT 23: SWINGS AND ROUNDABOUTS

137–38 "I John Locke, accompanied with": Richard Hakluyt, *The Principal Navigations, Voyages, Traffiques and Discoveries of the English Nation*, vol. 5 (Glasgow: James McLehose and Sons, 1904), 77, 87–88.

139 "millions of cats and hundreds of thousands": Donald W. Engels, *Classical Cats: The Rise and Fall of the Sacred Cat* (New York: Routledge, 2015), 152.

140 "certeine bookes of Cosmographie": Richard Hakluyt, *The Principal Navigations, Voyages, Traffiques and Discoveries of the English Nation*, vol. 1 (Edinburgh: E. & G. Goldsmid, 1885), 4.

141 "certaine blacke slaves": Richard Hakluyt, *The Principal Navigations, Voyages, Traffiques and Discoveries of the English Nation*, vol. 6 (Glasgow: James McLehose and Sons, 1904), 176.

INCIDENT 24: DESIGNATED DIVER

143–45 "*Thursday, July 11.*": Henry Fielding, *The Journal of a Voyage to Lisbon* (London: A. Millar, 1755), 87–90.

146 "The stories began to appear": Craig Chamberlain, "There Have Been a Lot of Cats in The New York Times, and Not All Just for Fun," *Illinois News Bureau* (blog), February 3, 2015, news.illinois.edu/blog/view/6367/204423.

146–47 Back in 1913, Ralph Pulitzer: Cassandra Tate, "What Do Ombuds-
men Do?" *Columbia Journalism Review* 23, no. 1 (May/June 1984): 37.

INCIDENT 25: EPITAPH

149–50 "To the memory of Trim": "Matthew Flinders' Biographical
Tribute to His Cat Trim."

150 "the man behind the map of Australia": Gillian Dooley, "Matthew
Flinders: The Man Behind the Map of Australia," *Transactions* (Royal
Society of Victoria blog), October 14, 2015, transactionsvic.blogspot
.com/2015/10/matthew-flinders-man-behind-map-of.html.

INCIDENT 26: PENGUIN BUDDIES

152–53 "[January 1821] After the loss of the *Cora*": Robert Fildes, "Journal
of a Voyage Kept on Board Brig 'Cora' of Liverpool Bound to New
South Shetland," 1820–21, typescript copy at Scott Polar Research
Institute, reference MS 101/1.

154 "No human can survive alone": David G. Campbell, *The Crystal Desert:
Summers in Antarctica* (Boston: Mariner Books, 2002), vii.

156 "a species of very large bird": "Important Discovery," *Imperial Magazine;
Or Compendium of Religious, Moral, and Philosophical Knowledge* 2, no. 18 (August
1820), 675.

156 "birds as big as ducks": "Penguins in History," Penguins-World,
penguins-world.com/penguins-in-history.

156–57 "We found two islands full of geese": Pigafetta, *The First Voyage Around
the World*, 49.

157–58 "Penguins are recent descendants": Campbell, *The Crystal Desert*,
79–80.

INCIDENT 27: GHOST SHIP

160–61 "A letter from Nassau, in the Bahamas": "A Ship Deserted," *Sailors'
Magazine* 7, no. 24 (December 1840), 383.

161 "I regret," reported Lloyds: *"Rosalie," Bermuda Triangle Central* (blog),
August 26, 2010, bermudatrianglecentral.blogspot.com/2010/08/
rosalie.html.

162 "scattered in an undisciplined fashion": Bland Simpson, *Ghost Ship of Diamond Shoals: The Mystery of the* Carroll A. Deering (Chapel Hill: University of North Carolina Press, 2002), 62.

162 "COAST GUARD WASHINGTON D.C.": Ibid., 11.

163 "Yes, I was here": Ibid., 221.

INCIDENT 28: CANNON CAT COLD CASE

165–66 "Bailing was now resumed": Francis B. Butts, "The Loss of the Monitor, by a Survivor," *Century Illustrated Monthly Magazine* 3, no. 2 (December 1885), 301.

167 "converted into a stock yard": "The Monitor After the Battle of Hampton Roads," Monitor National Marine Sanctuary, monitor.noaa .gov/150th/after.html.

INCIDENT 29: SOGGY, GROGGY MOGGIES

172 "The Sunday before Christmas": Robert Falcon Scott, *Scott's Last Expedition*, vol. 2 (New York: Dodd, Mead and Company, 1913), 256–57.

173 "the energy and elasticity of his movements": "Matthew Flinders' Biographical Tribute to His Cat Trim."

173–74 "In Sydney we had hauled out": Charles H. Ross, *The Book of Cats*, 289.

174 "It seemed utterly impossible": Alan Villiers, *The Cruise of the* Conrad (Dobbs Ferry, NY: Sheridan House, 2006), 320.

174 "the help of the galley stove": "The Future of Sailing Ships," *Lookout* 28, no. 11 (November 1937): 10.

INCIDENT 30: HARDTACK SAVES THE DAY

178 "biskit of muslin": "The Ship's Biscuit," Royal Museums Greenwich, rmg.co.uk/discover/explore/ships-biscuit.

178 "one pound daily of good, clean": Ibid.

179 "This stone was found wedged": "Portsmouth's Historic Dockyard: The Rock from HMS Pique," Memorials and Monuments in Portsmouth, memorialsinportsmouth.co.uk/dockyard/pique.htm.

179–80 "The only thing that ever really frightened me": In Gary
    Sheffield, "The Battle of the Atlantic: The U-Boat Peril," BBC, last
    updated March 20, 2011, bbc.co.uk/history/worldwars/wwtwo/battle_
    atlantic_01.shtml.

180 "of the smashed ships": Herbert Corey, "Ships Snatched from the
    Sea," *Nation's Business*, March 1943: 36.

MASCOTS
182 mascots "were part of the team": Arnold Arluke and Lauren Wolfe, *The
    Photographed Cat: Picturing Human-Feline Ties* (Syracuse, NY: Syracuse
    University Press, 2013), 111.

INCIDENT 31: SPICK-AND-SPAN
187 "Tom was wounded in one foot": Mrs. Charles D. Sigsbee, "Pets in the
    Navy," *St. Nicholas* 26, no. 1 (November 1898–April 1899): 63.

INCIDENT 32: TURNING TRICKS
190 "His exercises commenced": "Matthew Flinders' Biographical Tribute
    to His Cat Trim."

INCIDENT 33: UNDER FIRE
194 "We had a black and a tabby cat": "Podcast 34: Animals in War."

196–97 "When the war began": Alan Taylor, "World War I in Photos:
    Animals at War," *Atlantic*, April 27, 2014, theatlantic.com/
    photo/2014/04/world-war-i-in-photos-animals-at-war/507320.

INCIDENT 34: FIRST AID
198–99 "13 December 1919": US Navy Bureau of Medicine and Surgery,
    "Catnipped! The True Tale of Thomas Whiskers, USN," *Grog: The Journal
    of Navy Medical History and Heritage* (originally *Grog Ration*) 3, no. 2 (March–
    April 2008): 6. Republished with permission from Mr. André B.
    Sobocinski, historian, Communications Directorate, US Navy Bureau
    of Medicine and Surgery.

INCIDENT 35: THE REAL DEAL, OR TALL TALE CONSTRUCTION

208 "One of the crew happened to see Blackie": Anna Bemrose, *Mawson's Last Survivor: The Story of Dr Alf Howard AM* (Salisbury, Brisbane: Boolarong Press, 2011), 92.

INCIDENT 36: BRUSH WITH FAME

211 "Churchill restrains 'Blackie' the cat": "Winston Churchill as Prime Minister 1940–1945," Imperial War Museums, iwm.org.uk/collections/item/object/205195546.

211 "He should have conformed": "Churchill Should Pet Cat Only If Invited, Fans Say," *The New York Times*, September 23, 1941.

213 "The President of the United States": "The Atlantic Charter," North Atlantic Treaty Organization, last updated October 1, 2009, nato.int/cps/en/natohq/official_texts_16912.htm.

INCIDENT 37: RED LEAD

215 "Red Lead, ship's kitten": "Our Furry Recruits: Cats of War," Australian War Memorial, January 21, 2016, awm.gov.au/articles/blog/our-furry-recruits-cats-war.

215–17 "*Perth* was due to sail": Ronald McKie, *Proud Echo* (Sydney: Angus and Robertson, 1953), 4–5. Published in the United States as *The Survivors: The Story of the Gallant Fight of the Cruisers Perth and Houston Against Great Odds* (New York: Bobbs-Merrill, 1953).

INCIDENT 38: DISEMBARKING

219–20 "Detention of animals on board vessels in harbour": "Statutory Instruments 1974 No. 2211, Animals—Diseases of Animals, The Rabies (Importation of Dogs, Cats and Other Mammals) Order 1974," legislation.gov.uk/uksi/1974/2211/made/data.xht?wrap=true.

220 "In consequence of complaints made": "Sailors' Pets," *Mercury* (Hobart, Tasmania), May 5, 1908.

221 "A ship's cat has been saved": "Ships Laid Up in River Blackwater: Sagamore," Mersea Museum, merseamuseum.org.uk/mmvesseldetails.php?tot=411&typ=nam&pid=147&wds=&hit=356.

223 "All mascots had to be removed": Michael Wynd, "Mascots in the Navy," Navy Museum Research Inquiry (New Zealand), October 2013, pelorusjackblog.files.wordpress.com/2015/02/mascots-in-the-navy.pdf.

About the Authors

Bart may track his story back to a cat carved on a column in the sixteenth century, but scribe **PHILIPPA SANDALL** reckons her seafaring Norris forebears go back to Vikings who settled in Normandy and then headed to England and Hastings with William. So they say. Since then, there have been many seafarers in the family, numbers of whom have been lost overboard (and no one rowed to the rescue).

Illustrator **AD LONG** comes from a long line of landlubbers . . . though his earliest Australian ancestors sailed out in 1788 on board the First Fleet. She was a housemaid who stole the silver; her death sentence was commuted to imprisonment at the far end of the world. He was an Irish marine who made an honest woman of her. Together they raised a bunch of kids. And they raised cats, lots of cats.